BLESS THE BLOOD

a cancer memoir

WALELA NEHANDA

Kokila

Kokila

An imprint of Penguin Random House LLC, New York

First published in the United States of America by Kokila,
an imprint of Penguin Random House LLC, 2024

Copyright © 2024 by Walela Nehanda

Visit us online at PenguinRandomHouse.com.

Library of Congress Cataloging-in-Publication Data is available.

ISBN 9780593529492

1st Printing

Printed in the United States of America
LSCH

This book was edited by Sydnee Monday, copyedited by Kaitlyn San Miguel, proofread
by Robert Farren, and designed by Asiya Ahmed. The production was supervised by
Tabitha Dulla, Nicole Kiser, Ariela Rudy Zaltzman, and Caitlin Taylor.

Text set in Bookmania.

This is a work of nonfiction. Some names and identifying details have been changed.

This book is a living memory. It's the only way to say
I was here, we were here. My entire family.
This is for the names I do and do not know,
the ones who cover me: my ancestors.

I owe everything to you. This book is dedicated to us.

Dear Reader,

This book encapsulates a time in which I experienced many things that people would consider disturbing, triggering, overwhelming, or uncomfortable. It is my intent to shed light on what often feels unbearable to talk about.

Sometimes, when reading heavy words, you may feel seen in a way that can be both comforting and painful. Sometimes, when reading heavy words, you may be made aware of realities outside of your own that can be both enraging and jarring. Either way, witnessing a heavy journey such as my own is a task in itself.

Please take care in the ways you need while reading my book.

If that means walking away from this book for a week, a month, a year, or forever—so be it. If that means throwing this book against a wall, please do so—it was built for it. If that means crying into this book—my words will hold your tears; this ink was made to be blotted.

If at any point you feel overwhelmed, please call a friend or loved one to vent, talk to a trusted person in your life, partake in some sort of self-nourishing activity to soothe your nervous system, or reach out to whatever network you have, big or small, for support. Be gentle, sweet soul, with your heart, your emotional world, and your bodymind.

Content Warning: cancer, hospitalizations, medical procedures, medical racism, microaggressions, macroaggressions, ableism, chronic pain, stem cell transplant, systemic violence, physical and emotional abuse, neglect, sexual assault, suicidal ideation, self-injury, disordered eating, financial trauma, social media, substance use, chronic pain, medication, weapons, racism, classism, depression, anxiety, PTSD, neurodivergence, homophobia, misgendering, transphobia, fatphobia, erasure, death of loved ones, grief & loss.

writer's note: this here ain't a john green novel

after cynthia parker-ohene

look, before we get started, imma let y'all know: this here ain't a
john green novel. i do actually smoke down the cigarette augustus
waters puts between his teeth. i don't believe in corny Tumblr
metaphors about death. i will pick up that lighter. inhale marlboro
reds to the chime of funeral bells and an IV beeping. this is not a
romanticization of tragedy. no, there won't be a nicholas sparks
redemption arc reserved for me. i'm not an innocent porcelain
angel like jamie sullivan from *a walk to remember.* do not expect
me to perform infinite kindness or gratitude. notice black people
do not exist in these worlds, but cancer exists in mine and
theirs. again, this here ain't a john green novel. you 'bout to step
into my world. one of the misunderstood. this here ain't for the
hardheaded ego or faint of heart. i plan to fail any expectation
you have of me. there's no prophetic wisdom to sip in doses of
stanzas like a prescription. i am not an inspiration. i am not the
undesirable, ugly ghoul that society portrays the sick and black
and disabled to be. welcome to my lecture on medical racism.
i'm not here to make survival comfortable. i am indeed the bad
cancer patient. i talk back and think after. i cuss. i hold glorious
pity parties. i self-sabotage. i am the catchall for assumptions. i
am not your token negro. i will spit at the feet of those who spite
me. i am not part of white men's "robust" imagination where they
thread plot lines about lives they've never lived. i do not want to
be imagined by them. that's why you're here. reading this. there is

no consent in the "theatrics of cancer." there is no soft underbelly of the beast [america] for black folks. this book is a mess about time. and cancer. and time. and love. and time. and hurt. and time evading us all. no happy endings. it just. is. a witnessing.

Hopscotch for Leukemia
Was Apparently for a Real Disease

"You have a white blood cell count of 660,000.
That is 600 percent more than normal. You likely have leukemia.
You will be getting admitted to the oncology unit" flatlines the room

The doctor darts out as quickly as he says the news.
He leaves a nurse trying to hold back her pity but failing miserably.
My eyebrows twist into a question mark devoid of panic.
I don't know what leukemia is.
I haven't even heard of it.
Mmm, well, except this one time at Montessori.
In elementary school, we were competing in a fundraiser
for some poor, sick kids pictured in colorless pamphlets.
Eight hours passed to the metronome of hopscotching across
my school's pastel chalk concrete playground.
I was lighthearted back then.
Not whatever this is now—
my face slammed against the garage door of my mind.

A Google search illuminates me,

leukemia is: blood cancer
 . . .

Cannnceeerr . . . ???

ARE YOU BLEEPIN'
KIDDIN' ME,
CANCER!?!

Phase 3 CML Described like a Genre of Sci-Fi for the Sake of Your Understanding

The planet is Walela, Captain.
    The organisms are cells,
        bones, tissues, blood,
           and organs.

It is an unforgiving planet,
    unrestrained in nature already.
Harsh conditions have now encouraged the creation of mutants
destroying the planet:
    The mutant alien is the result of a DNA mismatch gone awry.
      The DNA mismatch creates a defective nonhuman cell.
        The nonhuman cell carries
        the rogue Philadelphia chromosome.
        That chromosome, sir,
        produces the genetic missile:
        BCR-ABL.

That gene decomposes the human cell into:
      a leukemic white blood cell.
      Nonhuman.
        Can procreate on its own,
        reproducing at a bizarrely rapid rate.
        Bubbling up into gargantuan
        charcoal slime gray aliens.

If the mutant aliens take over planet Walela,
we have a threat to the safety of humanity:
a Cancer Planet—
the terrain's skeleton will be shaved into sawdust.
These things will overcrowd the bone marrow,
pollute the planet's only water source:
blood.
Blood carries the alien's
sole source of transportation
to home base:
the bone marrow.

Captain, we cannot infiltrate sneakily like those cunning
bastards did.
The other organisms will die if we don't do something.
I suggest we stage a full-force attack:
leukapheresis, chemotherapy,
biopsies. Check.
Back-up laser cannons. Check.
Full-force chemotherapy,
total-body radiation lasers.
Starve the aliens of their
water source, transportation,
and home base. Check.

To ensure their extermination,
we will transfer healthy cells from a nearby planet
with an almost identical HLA makeup to planet Walela.
If Walela accepts, it will be a regeneration.

A recalibration making Walela a safe,
nonviolent planet.
The crew is flying into formation as I speak,
Captain—we are asking for permission to fire.

Symptoms of the Undiagnosed

Jackson Pollock splatter–painted legs.

Bones under thin skin,
a cymbal-clapping marching band.

Fatigue marked by labored breath.

A persistent cough.
Lungs rippling with infection.

Society claims it's my diet cuz
who can afford to be sick in this economy?
Nobody got that kind of cash.
Health is wealth.
Meaning white and rich.

Vision out my left eye split into a stuck film reel.

Vertigo mistaken for anxiety.
Headaches spill lava into my cranium.

Tiny red dots
congregate round bruises
to give a Sunday sermon.

Soaked bedsheets
explained as "night terrors."

A distended abdomen.
Rail-thin thighs.
Hair too stubborn to grow.

Everything's been hazy for a while now.
Been spending years wandering around
in this meat suit of a body. Hurtling myself
toward an inevitably late diagnosis.
They did not lie when they said:

Ignorance is bliss.

"Family Reunion" —The O'Jays

Leukemia speeds up a family reunion.
Last week, we mediated awkwardness
with homemade spaghetti. My fiancée,
Ivie, even got a birthday gift from Mom.
It's been a slow reconciliation with good reason.
Too bad cancer hates lollygagging.
Throws me the phone and shouts, *"Catch!"*
I do not want to dial the number
because that means I need them.
"Yeah, Dad, I'm at the hospital,
they think I have cancer.
"Oh no, okay, I'll call Mom."
Mom's at her twelve-hour shift today,
short for: do not bother her for a thing.
"You better be turning blue," she'd always say
—I observe my forearms, not blue, just leukemic.
"I mean, it's okay if she can't come,
I know she's been busy."
She's also seen worse.

      Excuses and reasons for my mother
      to not give a damn boomerang
      any self-regard I once had
      out the hospital room door.
I repeat her mantra:
"Don't make your unpreparedness my emergency."
      The forewarning to not inconvenience her.

And she's right:

Prior Preparation Prevents Piss-Poor Performance.

I was the one who didn't go to the doctor sooner.

I wasn't responsible enough.

I should've stopped and listened harder.

Then *I* wouldn't be here in this mess to begin with.

The Mirage After Diagnosis

I look outside the same
door the ER doc exited.

A kid is on the other side.
Got her hair slicked back
into a thick black ponytail
swinging high with each skip.
She's decked out in medium-
washed denim jeans,
a bright scarlet shirt.
Gap-toothed, wide-mouthed,
and boisterous.

She freezes as our lives pass each other.
Observant, she notices the desolation.
The blood as melted brown candle wax
smeared atop blankets from a botched IV.
A loose baby-blue gown hangs off my shoulders.
Our thick black hair chopped short.
She was taught to be polite,
so she waves in a rush, longing to forget me.

I have become my own nightmarish terror.
Heard the word *leukemia*,
then saw everyone's damp coffee-
stained promises sweep out the room.

I seal my eyelids to the sound of a dial tone.
Call up Delusion's home. *"I don't know
what the hell a white blood cell count 600 percent
more than normal is. Just fix it,"* I say nonchalantly.

I am unable to understand how I was taught
to make a game of illness as a child.

A cool-toned voice sneers,
*"We never think about mortality
until it's staring out from underneath
the Reaper's hood, tallying life
on a chalkboard,
calling out your name.
Next."*

The Mentor's Silence

after the news,
i message my mentor on facebook

i have cancer and can't perform at the LA poetry festival

he reads it
and

.

.

.

is silent

silence
is an acknowledgment of its own kind:

"i do not care what you are going through,"
or
"i am afraid of mortality and you smell like it,
so i got the message and felt the clock start ticking.
i had to make you a byproduct of my imagination.
you are the clay on a wheel i spin. i weld together
a vase of empty platitudes that i will only practice
in the mirror but never to your face,"
or
the silence says,
"i would die if i went through the same thing.

you got this tenacity growling in a forest of dying trees.
you and the cancer hold hands and become demons,
how do you live with darkness inside you?
what did you do to get that?
got that thang on you,
i gotta will you away like a curse."

The Stench

He's not wrong
about the whole
stench-of-mortality thing.
The hospital,
its smell,
it follows you everywhere.
It is not of this world,
but of two realms
colliding:
the unalive
and living dead.

You don't understand sacrifice
or the weight of expectation until

you are likely dying and everyone
in the room knows it and everyone
in the room thinks *you* don't know it.

Hushed whispers on the other side
of tissue-paper curtains don't conceal
the hospital being bleak and morose.

To create a diversion, you crack dry jokes,
invent a *Parent Trap* handshake with the oncologist.
Pep up and engage in small talk with nurses.
Encourage your fiancée to take selfies with you.
Let everyone cry into your shoulder
or hand or at your bedside.

Your family will call you *baby*.
Claim they are scared.
There will be even more family,
cousins who you have not seen
or spoken to in years.
They will sing with jokes,
making everything seem less
                    . . . real.

Open your phone to messages
from people you once hated,
now apologizing to alleviate
their own consciousness
just in case you do, you know, die.

You say sorry too.

Send your own apology messages
to alleviate your consciousness
just in case you do, you know, die.

You want to, no, you need to
make sure everyone knows
you are okay.
No, not just okay,
that you are at peace.
Even if you are suffocating
from within the plastic bag
of your own fear.
You need those you love
to be able to remember
a truth you've concocted,
a remedy for their healing:

Walela . . . was happy,
they felt . . . little to no pain,
they died . . . fighting,

looked like their newborn photo:
black unruly hair combed down,
fists up, scowling,
prepared for whatever
it meant arriving
Earthside.

Leukapheresis

A Quinton catheter slips into my neck.
Lines connect me to a machine handing
over all the dirty blood I been hoarding.
I am told my blood is filling cloudy brown bags.
The easiest way to describe leukapheresis is:
a cleansing, a detox of sorts.
Eviction notices sent to excess
white blood cells alongside
nine oral chemotherapy pills.
The other two bags,
apparently holding my blood too,
are stained a Kool-Aid red. The good blood
recirculating from my neck
into the reservoir of my veins.
No matter what, it's all me:
Dirty // Clean—Bad // Good
My white blood cells dwindle.
For six days,
I throw up into a bag.
I am indeed
a toxic. soiled.
piece of shit.

My Mother Asks, "What Do You Want to Have Happen If You Die?" and We Sign the Advanced Directive

This is not my body's first time trying to kill itself.
I remember back when Hope first manifested
as a jagged piece of glass in an alley
off Vermont and Jefferson two years ago,
when I thought my blood was a cancer.
I was a liar to those I loved
and tried to drain myself empty
because the Shame is unsurvivable,
and suicide felt like the answer for
everyone to be without the stress
of my craziness.

Now the Past holds the Present captive,
and now my blood really is a cancer
except this time I don't want to die
—at least I don't think.
All these years of people telling me,
"If you believe something long enough,
it'll come true," so of course
Irony mocks me when the cancer
diagnosis makes an anvil of itself.
I tell Irony to shut the entire hell up
even though I beckoned this arrival.

Wished for Death so many times
that, of course, when I forgot his name
—he sent the vultures for my carcass.

In the hospital, my mother asks me
where I want to be buried,
if it'll be above my grandmother
at the Inglewood Park Cemetery.
Irony inserts herself again
—cackles at a mother asking
her own child about their funeral.

Faith sits still in the corner,
holding hands with Doubt,
and I question: maybe if I never
lied about being sick when I was younger
or tried to manipulate love out of people
like squeezing a dried orange rind
—maybe this wouldn't have happened.
This is the "what goes around
comes around" part and I do deserve it.

But Reason tells me
it's so much deeper than that,
and Fate nods his head in agreement,
and God is puffing on a cigar
in the corner of my hospital room,
with his feet kicked up in the easy chair, asking
how bad I want to stay or leave.

Remorse makes me believe I don't know
the answer. Guilt asks I talk to Lucifer instead.
I say I don't want to die, and my grandmother's
voice reminds me how melancholic I've always been
—even as a child. That Home is a place
where sadness don't exist. And all the gospel songs
I've spent my whole life listening to speak of a heaven
we spend life marching toward—I say this all don't sound
so bad. That either way this goes, it's a survival of some kind,
that either way this goes, I did ultimately survive myself
so I don't clutch on to Hope's hand so heavy,
whisper, "Thy will be done"
and Nina swings from the chandelier
singin', "Freedom is living without fear"
and Irony laughs again.
Except this time, I join in.

For a moment,
the hospital bed is just a bed.
My tubes, jewelry.
This makeshift gown,
a ballroom gown with a chiffon train.
I dance with my grandaddy,
who passes me to Ivie,
and I dance with Ivie,
who returns me to myself,
and I waltz in circles alone
on the border between
Heaven & Earth.

My Fiancée, Ivie, and I Open Our Memory Box In My Hospital Room

Two ripped tickets for *Star Trek* in July at Pacific Theatres.
It was part of the date I had planned for us.
We took the bus to Hollywood; you got an Africa tattoo
    on your wrist.
Then we booked it on the 217 to Umami and bronzed on
    the outdoor patio.
The movie was an excuse to make out in the last row
until we got so tired and slept on each other's shoulders.

The first engagement ring after two weeks of dating:
    a smooth amethyst
rolled into rose-gold wiring from Leimert Park's Sunday
    drum circle.
I was already bejeweled, but we went to a jeweler off
    Pershing Square.
Lusted over a chocolate diamond and said after ten years together,
maybe we could afford that. I didn't need to stare at the glass
    windows for long.
A gold band with small diamonds on either side of
    a garnet gemstone.
There. That's the one.

Two red Afropunk Festival wristbands. A bus ride in matching
    berets to New York.
Swaying hips to The Internet's "Get Away" live. Dirt from the
    ground kicked up
and slicked across everyone's bodies oozing with promise.
    We spent the night
with boys from my one semester in college who are why
    I do poetry.
Lighting up cigarettes, we surprised everybody with
    me growing up.

My granny's gold elephant ring. The two of us on a bench in
    Malcolm X Park,
huddled over your phone's speaker playing Chance the Rapper's
    "Juke Joint."
I leaned in to kiss you, fished out the box. *Will you marry me too?"*

One hot-pink MAKE OUT NOT WAR sticker from
    Prophets of Rage,
the summer we met, 2016, protesting the Los Angeles
    Police Department.

An expired limited-edition Metro TAP card. You had brought
    me to your neighborhood,
where one of your elders told us to name our nonexistent
    future child Fidel.

Egyptian musk and a two-dollar bill for luck.

The first poem I wrote for you. Etched into the back of some
   notebook paper,
a secret *Please don't ever leave me.* Hand-printed between
   lead pencil and baby-blue lines.

Unfortunately, a Formal Diagnosis of Leukemia Requires a Bone Marrow Biopsy

Stomach down.
Lower back
exposed
as a slab
of thick
stubborn
Concrete.

The biopsy needle
is not a needle
but a construction drill.
Lidocaine don't mean
a thing when it comes
to cutting a perfect circle,
inserting a twenty-two gauge
needle, aspirating liquid like
a turkey baster out my bones,
all to be collected for testing.
I do not scream,
I bite the insides of my cheeks
like when my parents yelled at me.

I learned in high school,
pain is what your mind makes of it.
My eyes scan the hospital room door.
Outside, Disassociation and Denial
fight over who gets to enter my room
first.

The First Set of Seven Days

A touch-deprived past will create an overcompensating adult. But in the hospital, I do not have to be hypervigilant for once. For the first time since elementary school, my mother sits in bed with me. Hugs me and pecks a kiss on the top of my forehead. Steely facades rust into history when her finger traces my face. She hadn't done that since I would be laid up on her bed after school. She would be watching soap operas like *General Hospital* or *Dr. Phil,* or a Tyler Perry play would have her hollering. She'd simultaneously be picking the acne off my face until my father would swing open the front door from his long day at work or my homework was stacking too high for the evening. Intimacy between mother and child had always been this restrained give-and-take. In the hospital, though. Well, rephrase. In the hospital and when I may be dying, my mother feels like . . . a mother. Ensures I am receiving the best care possible. Takes notes of everything the doctors say. Assists with dragging my feet into a stride, encourages me to get up each day, because I desperately need to be moving. Helps me change my gown and use the bedpan (yeah, never thought we'd get that close either). Cleans my Quinton catheter and bone marrow biopsy sites, checking for infection. My hair all matted from days going unkempt. She cradles my neck like a newborn's. Steadily lowers my head under a faucet of warm water. Wraps me in a towel. Takes a comb, works through my hair, and ties a pink bandana over it. *"You know I'd give my life for you, right?"*

i guess i've experienced salvation

On the oncology unit floor,
my nickname is "the Baby."
I'm the youngest patient by a long shot,
making me the most interesting to talk to.
Nurses take extra time (if they can) in my room.
The night before I'm discharged,
one of them and I chat in lowered voices,
keeping Ivie from waking in the cot beside me.
"Yeah, you know everybody was surprised
you could walk into the ER with that high
of a count, and now it's 54,000."
I did not fully comprehend how much tugging
my body was resisting. Like. Organ failure.
Stroke. Sudden death. She peers over at me
with disbelief. Flushes the IV. *"Your oncologist*
was right, you've got to have done some really
good things to have come out of this.
Welcome to your second life." Tonight, I die.
Tomorrow, I am Jesus on Palm Sunday.
This year it falls on my grandmother's birthday.
A resurrected miracle Returning home.

The Family Home Rules Described to Me, at 23 Years Old, before Discharge

1. No more poetry

2. No more activism

3. No one cares about your illness on the internet

4. No social media posts about 1, 2, 3

5. Your name is [insert dead name]

6. You're a Christian

7. None of this hoodoo-voodoo nonsense anymore

8. A binding contract is the guarantee of long-term love

9. Love is bought: bedding and clothing and food and transportation to the hospital / Negotiate: yourself / The other party: not required to

10. Cancer makes you our second chance to conceive the daughter we always wished for

11. Nowhere is ever safe. What's the phrase? The hell you know is better than the one you don't?

12. We want you to move back in. We really do. But, sign here, [not on your terms] first.

My Childhood Home

An Anthropologie candle flicks the scent of cashmere and linen.

Our entryway, black and wooden checkerboarded, worn down
from my shoe scuffs in preschool through high school.
The living room is a U-turn from the entryway.
One step down, a crown-molded fireplace Santa slid out of.
The extra space I used to wear only socks and ballerina spin
or follow workouts from *Seventeen* magazine.

A narrow hallway leads to the master bedroom,
my mother's small walk-in closet with mocha-brown carpet.
Before the master bedroom, an office with three desks,
where I once did my homework. A thick bleached swinging
door into the kitchen. Lace curtains allow a patterned daylight
to shine on our circular kitchen table. Dinner with Mom and Dad,
with our family's whiteboard hanging to the left—Expo markers
in blue for Mom's workdays, green for me, red for my father.
My dad's spaghetti, shrimp scampi, or Cuban black beans
and rice were made on our fifties-style stove. Other nights
    it was ordering
in from Natalee Thai or Chin Chin or the Chinese to-go spot down
the street by my family's favorite nail salon off Pico and La Cienega.

An archway to step through. A white washer and dryer
sit beside each other. My mom taught me early how to clean,

separate clothes into loads, instructed the science behind
laundry soap and fabric softener to a pair of tiny hands.

The back door opens to three steps leading down to a
    concrete driveway.
Magenta hibiscus bushes line the right side and bloom in the spring.
This is where I learned to skateboard and raced my friends
    back and forth.
Swing a left in the driveway and a patch of grass with a lemon and
an orange tree. Oranges would fall and my mother would
    stop me from
eating them. Left them as offerings for the squirrels,
    the small beings
had homes here too. Scurrying from our trees and
    visiting our windows.
Someone always had a place to sleep and food in their belly.
That don't guarantee peace, but it's enough.

The Second Set of Seven Days

When I'm discharged, my mom helps me into the house and settles me into the mud-brown living room easy chair. My former creature comfort where I used to spend every weekend with my feet kicked up, reclined and watching *Grey's Anatomy*. She prepares my favorite tuna sandwich from her homemade lunch boxes of the past and helps me into my bedroom to nap under a cloud duvet cover. She checks in on me periodically, asks about how I'm feeling physically but also emotionally. She's empathetic, she's loving, she smiles at me, and it feels like she means it. Like she really sees I've grown up and she can love me as an adult she respects versus a child in need of controlling.

Irony Tells One More Joke

Hobbling with
a biopsy site
slicing bone.
Wounds
are more
than physical,
such as:
my mother's
smirk,
a salt mine
fizzling,
"See,
I told you,
you were always
going to need me
before
I needed
you."

The novelty of cancer is wearing off

& if anything, it is proving to be
annoying for everyone.

My mother no longer smiles at me.
Her anger about what does not have
to do with me festers in a room
full of sores. Eggshells cover the hallway
& "how are you doing" is an afterthought.

Her annoyance whips at my lethargy.
Her annoyance flares when I am absent-minded,
when I leave a pair of socks on the ground.
Back when I was a kid, if I did that,
I'd get grounded.
Now? Over eighteen?
Chastised.

You're crying?
Well, you can leave.
There's the door.

Can I, though?

Is it willingly?

Or am I fleeing?

"Will I" Sung by the 2008 Cast of the Broadway Production of *Rent*

Normal doesn't exist.
Normal stopped when I got diagnosed.
Too many people want the kid
from April 10, 2017, who stumbled
into the ER with Ivie.
I thought we all agreed
that person died in *that* hospital,
emerged on a Palm Sunday and, Holy Jesus,
was named the eighth wonder of the world.
After that, Normal was no longer
a vocabulary choice.
Like in fourth grade,
when my mother and father agreed
I couldn't say the word *provoke*.
The people I love show me:
love is transactional.
I must become the someone
they know,
who *they* want me to be,
as *their* cancer patient,
as *their* disabled adult child.
It is never about me, it never was,
not once is it considered
how I wanted to experience this trauma.

Can you lend me some space, man?
I'm tryna figure things out for a second.
Stop telling me, start asking me:
How do you want to live
with some dignity?

Two Versions of Myself Split Off and
Meet in My Childhood Bedroom

The pictures of me are all destroyed,
but my winding childhood bed frame remains.
The window—still off-kilter
from the nights I'd sneak out
with men too old
to be waiting outside for me.
The room still has my cream-
colored cabinets with olive-
green trimming and oil-painted
pink roses. This room is a living exhibition.
A museum:
Insert: me Now // Exit: me Then
Two beings, at odds, encircling each other
like koi fish trapped in a tar pond.
[insert dead name] is a retirement plan who belongs to her parents.
Long, wavy blonde hair to her waist thanks to Sun In
    and chlorine pools.
A smile chiseled from practice in the mirror, repeating
    she wants to be a doctor
until it is believable. A placeholder for her parents' aspirations.
    An American
Girl doll in a Catholic-school uniform, and the men still catcall—
"Oops! . . . I Did It Again" is their perverted fantasy.

Fetishizing a young

girl, but yikes, they don't note: the textured beaded
   bracelets forming

a pattern to obscure a knife's cat scratches. Note: Did you
   see her eat?

How about sleep? Does she tell you she busies herself
   with ideas of love

saving her from her father's indifference and mother's
   emotional neglect?

Does she tell you how she's internalized her consciousness?

But she's so well manicured. So well spoken. So mature
   for her age.

Her parents malleating her life into a silver platter for
   a bourgeois dream.

Praying she'll marry into an elite family, like the Kennedys
   or the Kissingers,

pop out some grandkids under the pseudonym of Dr. [insert

                                    dead name

                                        here].

I, on the other hand, do not belong to my parents.

Disowned by my father's scowl.
Stood in a driveway holding
two trash bags with clothes
and my first teddy bear that
has since been lost. Tattooed
Hell Hath No Fury
across my stomach &
that was the strike my father
used, condemning me into exile.
My mother made to believe
I left without saying goodbye.
Her fits of resentment destroyed
most of my art and photographs.
Evocation sours my scars.
The tattoos covering my arm made
raw again. I am the college dropout.
The "tortured" artist. Surfer of homes.
Softhearted but had to be ruthless often.
But there is someone who loves me,
for real this time, in spite of all of it.
And that is enough to validate my agency.
Can say proudly that I am not my family's crest,
but I'm polishing one of my own with Ivie.
Falling under duvet covers, I spy a dose
of bright blue liquid resting on my bedside table.

It is placed neatly between medications
and liquid multivitamins—a "Welcome Home."
"Remember to Follow the Rules."
I roll my eyes.
It's the goddamn matrix in here.

"Like Rock & Roll and Radio" — Ray LaMontagne

Mama would take a small black boom box
and sit it up on the bathroom counter playing KJLH.
102.3 The Beat. Gospel if it was Sunday.
Her meditation after working twelve hours in a day.
Placed the pink plastic rollers in a worn-out Target bag.
Hot-curled her hair, tied each strand intricately
until her head was covered in tomorrow's unraveling.
She'd call me into the room with her.
I'd sit on top of the toilet cover,
and she'd either snap me into shape
just by a look in the mirror or tell me
a story about her mama or me as a baby.
There was laughter, though. Always laughter.
She'd run a bath, fill it with bubbles,
a series of melting icebergs.
She'd wipe the day off her as steam rose
and fell. I never could curl or wrap my hair properly,
no matter how many times I followed each stroke meticulously.
Not all things that are magic announce themselves boldly.
Sometimes, it's a Black mother and child making it to evening.
Resting.

Family of Spies

In fourth grade,
I brought my father in for show-and-tell.
Other kids had their pet rabbits, puppies,
and most prized possessions like vintage
sports trading cards, but I dragged my father in.
The year is 2003 and *Spy Kids* has a choke hold
on the greater elementary school population.
My father was a real spy, though. Not that whimsical
movie crap. He was the real deal.
Was a teenager in East Germany,
decoding messages over sound waves
for a double agent. A man on both sides
of the Stasi and CIA. My oma, the other woman.
The mistress caught up in a secret 007 affair.
The promise of love as freedom will
make you lose your mind and safety.
I am sure reminding him of being a teenager
with a bounty on his head
and a firing squad chomping at his heels
is more traumatizing than he lets on.
But he complies. This is parenthood, I guess.
He has a different name now.
One he was forced to choose.
But it's the one he passes down when I am born.
Pats my head when I ask in front of everyone,
"Were you a spy?" while handing out

German candy from a nearby deli.
He replies, "Sort of. I was half a spy, dear."
I triumphantly look at my classmates
and their bewildered faces, squeal,
"Then that makes me a quarter spy!"
True, I'm sure he didn't ever imagine
this was the life he'd choose. But for a time,
we were stuck together. Against all odds.
Like it was fate to have found the other.

The Early 2000s Weren't as Liberal as Everyone Claims

That same year,
I had my first standardized test
where race and ethnicity
became a car ride debate.
"There's no bubble for 'other,'
but I'm not just Black
and I'm not just White,"
I ponder aloud in the
back of my dad's car.
My mother snaps,
"You don't pass no brown
paper bag test.
If you got a drop of Negro,
then You are Black.
That is how the world sees you.
You are Black.
No White Person Gon Claim You."
My father's eyes avoid mine.
His silence, an incantation.
His wordlessness,
a premonition of its own.

An Invisible Orb Is Prescribed a Treatment Plan

My mom and oncologist sit in his office,
bouncing ideas for treatment plans between each other—
my mother speaks his language, that of the medical field,
one I am still learning. No one bothers to translate
as they talk percentage chances of this route vs. this route
vs. this route and the probability each would have
on the extension of my life—not one is higher than 20 percent.

The word *transplant* is uttered, and it hovers for a mere second
before it is swatted by my mother and the oncologist alike.
My mother's voice more fearful than anything.
I cannot understand what a transplant has to do
    with blood cancer.
All my questions won't collaborate with my mouth.
I don't like being told what to do.
But who knows what to do at twenty-three?
Who plans their lives with such caution?
—But I can't plan my life
—we are planning treatment.
I'm still tryna get a handle on all this.
Treatment is not my life,
but it is how I keep my life.

I stretch my legs,
stare out the window behind my oncologist's desk.

It overlooks the roundabout I got picked up from
   after being discharged.
I don't know anything, so I accept everything prescribed,
including my future: oral chemotherapy,
TASIGNA, highest dosage possible,
stay on standby for your cancer to comply.
Note: This pill is not a curative process.
Your cancer is you now.
But something is better than nothing.
I don't know any better or if there is anything better.
I am discussed without acknowledgment.
I've always been a nobody. A ceiling fan whizzes in my ears.
Everything is meaningless. I am soundproof foam,
an invisible orb floating in a clinical room.

the first oral chemotherapy: TASIGNA

yellow pills in punch packets to be swallowed twice a day.

strawberry-pink rashes splash against my forehead.

nausea rides a slide between my esophagus and stomach.

600 mg of Tylenol offsets the headaches.

a timer at six a.m. and one at six p.m. dings.

a dinner bell for my finicky leukemia.

the last supper: a painting

nailed into the cathedral

walls of my bones.

ivie and i make monuments memorializing
my childhood neighborhood

The #7 Big Blue Bus stop on my corner is gone. My street corner not enough of a landmark like the Vons up the street. Ivie takes the Metro Expo train and bus to see me, which takes forty-five minutes on a good day. My biopsy site hasn't been healing that great, and I thought walking was hard enough in the hospital, but Mom says I gotta move and keep moving.

Physical therapy was at first walking around the corner to Hansen's Cakes. A small shop with a gallery of tiered sample cakes for everything from weddings to children's birthdays, the walls decorated with celebrity headshots signing off with praises that this cake shop was their favorite cake shop, from the Kardashians to that one guy who plays in *The Terminator.* My parents got married with a Hansen's cake; every birthday cake I've ever eaten in my home has been a Hansen's cake. Vanilla frosting with pink-and-blue-frosting roses. The cake itself: vanilla with strawberry or chocolate creme. I bring Ivie into the shop where the workers know me, well, they know my mom, and by extension me, then run into the small bakery with cupcakes next door so I can taste being a kid again.

On the walk back, I point to different homes: "There was a man here and he died, but no one knew it until the whole building started to smell. I can't imagine dying that way, it's so sad." Or I point to a "beautifully refined home" and bring up how it once was owned by an artist and back then, the house had character. Wasn't trying to be something it wasn't. The place was a vibrant, rainbow-graffiti art installation in itself. I'm not joking when I say the house looked like it was actually spray-painted. I name the streets I used as shortcuts to get to major streets that no one knew about, especially the streets leading to my family's favorite Starbucks. In the same mini mall as a Shakey's Pizza and phone store. Starbucks was my first stop before going to school many mornings—the order: tall nonfat iced vanilla latte, three packets of Splenda, with an old-fashioned donut. I was on the way to my high school graduation early to practice my commencement speech, but I needed coffee so bad and it could've been a potentially regrettable decision in an all-white dress, but we managed. The neighborhood houseless folks saw me that day and talked about me being "yea high" years ago, running in front of the 7-Eleven down the street.

Everyone bore witness to me, like Bola, an older Indian man who knew my mom when she was a child, meaning he's known me since I was an infant and through my adolescent years consisting of 7-Eleven Slurpee obsessions. *"He always talked about wanting to take me to India and experience a traditional wedding; did you know they last for two weeks? That's what he said. You all will have to meet one day. I haven't seen him in so long."*

The neighborhood kids down the street are all grown now, but at one point in time we talked to one another. Nobody matched Josh. Josh was my neighborhood big brother. I excitedly told Ivie about the day she'd have to meet him. His parents became my "other grandparents" after my grandma and granny died. Him and his friends would scare the newer white neighbors who thought a crowd of young Black men talking outside in broad daylight was a disturbance of the peace. But also don't let me walk home from school and be followed by men adultifying a Black child because that is when you'd regret turning onto my block. That's the thing about being Black, even in neighborhoods that become whitewashed— the ones who stay behind still don't escape harassment.

When we get home, Ivie falls victim to a carb-induced nap on my family's dark-blue denim couch. I sit and read the Bible because I know that will make my mother content while she is at work. I am still debating about religion. Even after a near-death experience, faith being rejuvenated does not mean I invest myself in Christianity. But I also cannot help but notice the hospital I was able to walk out of has the same name as my childhood church. Some coincidences are not to be overlooked, so I indulge in theology. I get up and debate with Ivie to distract me from the tiredness that comes with walking farther distances.

Now we walk the opposite direction of Hansen's and down past a line of empty shops on Pico that once employed people in the neighborhood. I tell Ivie stories walking along each side of the street, like how one time I was FaceTiming on this exact crosswalk and my phone got snatched out of my hand by a kid on a bike. I tried to race him, almost grabbed on to his backpack, but a pedestrian red light made me lose him. Ivie teases at how naive I can be and it's true; for the most part, I think everyone is good. I try to. Because I've been an entire red flag whipping in the wind. I'm not how I once was growing up here. It's all different now, hints and flashes of an old life is what I chase during our walks. My youth seems to be outrunning me at every street corner; I'm too outta breath to keep up like I used to.

The Third Set of Seven Days

Another seven days pass; my dad sees my lab results while
    we walk my family's dog.
His smile is pressed into a thin line and asks without
    looking at me,
"So when are you moving out?"
"I thought you all wanted me to stay, like we were going
    to be a family again."
My mother interjects when we enter the front door,
    chuckles sarcastically.
"You must be confused. This was only temporary."

Sarcasm and psychological games are the warning shots
    before the yelling begins.
My anticipation moves like clockwork. The next day she
    yells about how I didn't
text where I went after being kicked out. The phone works
    both ways, and she never
checked about where in all of LA County I wound up.
    Whose couches and beds
I was sleeping in. Honesty about my abusive upbringing
    has my family
playing sympathy games, woe-is-me theatrics, and
    the gaslighting kindles.

Tenth-grade algebra, a teacher took my phone because
    my mother was texting so much.

I had made her mad again about something I can't remember
    now because the list
never ends. *Bzz bzz bzzz bzzzz bzzz bzzzzzzzzzzz.* Text
    messages inside my backpack
reading: *you make me sick, sick, sick* alongside photos
    of vomit and feces.
My phone is seen as a distraction to the class; the vibrations
    become a beat of their own,
in sync with the pulsating inside my throat. A cage for
    my own agitation.
The teacher does not question who is texting me.
I still wish she would have asked what the distraction was.
My mother working me double time:
in class managing Ivy League aspirations mixed with
    racial microaggressions
vs. my mother on the other end of an iPhone requiring me
    to manage her
emotions and expectations.

I'm grown now, but she, still the same, throws a tantrum
    for an apology.
My father, who is still the same, gives me the silent treatment
    for an apology.
I want one first. They say it in exasperation . . . like
    a rushed formality.
As if I'm asking for something ridiculous. Like. Respect.
Like. Reciprocity. Like. Compassion. *This is love, right?*

A Sarcastic Blessing for the First Man Who Complimented My Early Leukemia Symptoms, 2015

He showers in the room next door
while I start dressing myself.
Struggling to fit into my black-
and-white converse from high school,
I am distracted by the view outside his
window overlooking Wilshire Blvd.
Los Angeles's traffic ushers in the evening.
A man, eleven years older than me, from Tinder,
envisions I am some woman he loves in San Francisco.
I've latched my flesh onto his all summer,
wishing I was more than an exit for his mourning.
On the Uber ride home, wiry Apple headphones
play "So Special" by MUNA. Unrequited yearning
is inescapable, so I keep going back to him.
Believing if this ritual continues,
I will be worthy of a relationship.
But this is a man consumed
by making me into the keeper of his woes.
Momentarily, he stills with a double take.
Says: *"You're thinner,"*
pinching my withering waist.
Fat eaten by a lethal illness did not matter—

I was proud.

Desirability picks its teeth with a wooden stick,

and the belly fat of a twenty-one-year-old

falls off like good barbecue to him.

A Sarcastic Blessing for the Second Man Who Complimented My Early Leukemia Symptoms, 2016

This one lies atop a mattress bed in an Eagle Rock apartment.
Holding me in a way that only one other man from Hartford
has—like I'm worthwhile. Like maybe he'll stay longer.
A friend turned lover drifts asleep alongside me.
Wakes up, softly sweeps his hand across my stomach,
mentions how much better I would look if the tightening
of muscle occurred *there*: points to the slight lower
belly fat, the fat that will never leave me
(or most people for that matter).
I fix him a plate of myself, though.
Work out on the elliptical to Beyonce's *Lemonade*.
Lift weights like she did for Jay-Z.
Gosh, men can be foolish
believing they have the right to architect
anyone else around them.
Desperation for "romance"
makes a fool out of me.
It takes my second time at the gym
for the bruises to surface.
Unbeknownst to me,
cancer cells surf my bloodstream,
blasting brown skin into purple,
blue, green, yellow fireworks.
Punching, begging for escape

with bulging hematomas.
Spoiler: We don't fall in love.
He left upon finishing his last platter.
We both knew the night.
Scathing poems from me
finding the enemy target in him:
Everyone clapping. Us standing,
separated by a long wooden banquet table.
Both bitter. Anticipating the taste of bad
blood in goblets forged from animosity.

The Cancer Support Group

Nine older women sit in a semicircle.
The room's ambience is designed
to be soothing, but
I am a bull flaring its nostrils.
I am a handful and impatient.
Each woman sits in the beige-colored room
lamenting cancer or their childhood.
What could've gone right,
how cancer made them more grateful.
I am the angsty twentysomething-year-old.
But. They are not intimidated by me
nor are they surprised when the facade
melts into tears. Me. Sobbing.
Reading a poem about my grandma.
Talking about death, how I am not afraid of it,
and I'm not sure if that should be concerning.
The women call me wise. I laugh.
For it was a woman their age
who taught me to be like this.
I call myself a grandma
because I find most home with elders.
Elders who are willing to just let people
be people. Elders who understand anger
and sadness can coincide with joy.
That I am Pompeii,
ancient and a threat,

but easily turned to ash.
That I can be the biggest natural
disaster or the Earth healing.
These women slowly teach me
what it means to be gently volatile.

Concept: *Coraline* but Make It Black

The story goes:

My mother never allows me to be seen as an adult.

My father despises me and puppeteers my mother.

My poetry embarrasses the family into depression.

My mother denies depression and trades it in for

    the taste of blood.

My father denies depression and trades it in for earplugs.

Rage chases me to my lover's home.

Ivie's mother fashions herself into a new mother.

This one offers a home: Degnan

Home is wherever Ivie is and This Home

is petitioned as a pathway to "healing."

A place away from my mother.

Days pass. My mother barely calls.

Oncology appointments pass.

Interest from her wanes.

Her punishment has my self-worth goin' missing.

My self-worth is being inquired about on cartons

of milk at the Albertsons off Crenshaw and King.

Am I even halfway decent enough to be someone worth finding?

I have to be ain't shit if my mother chooses to be a bystander

to the assassin living inside me.

Ivie's mother, a bystander to my deterioration.

I want to shave my head and change into a different body,
one with buttons for eyes so I don't gotta acknowledge my
loneliness. Instead, Ivie's mother drives us to Target, and I
wander to the self-abandonment aisle drenched in cobalt dye.

The Starbucks off Crenshaw & Expo

is the work-study meet-up spot.
It's only three of us: me, Ivie,
and Stevie. We take up the
circular table by the barista bar.
Older Black men play newspaper
crossword puzzles. A Black woman
in lemon-yellow scrubs just got off work
and corrals her two girls in line to pick a snack.

It's quiet noise, a comforting kind.

When I was younger,
I used to be up in the Mid City Starbucks all day.
Would observe the absolute ordinary, the mundane.
Would imagine who the guy at the counter was
texting or wonder how long the inseparable
couple out the corner of my eye
have *actually* been together.

Cafés hold routine in a way that's stable to me.

Work-study is the same. Same date, same time.
Thursday evenings. Reading in close quarters,
slurping iced matcha green tea out of soggy
biodegradable straws. We cram words together in margins
as notes on printed PDFs.

Today it's *We Are Our Own Liberators*.
Ivie teaches about history and ideas
and how to make an idea into more
than just an idea but tangible plans
to try and change something from
our little corner of the coffee shop.

My Wedding Vows for Ivie—Just in Case:

You, my greatest teacher,
gatekeeper to the estate of myself.
We, a hurricane in Santa Monica
—a miracle of sorts.
Two children of Assata
and Kwame long stolen
from our homeland.

I think of all the elders
who tell us, "Liberation
is through struggle."
And by God, how we both
struggled to reach the
moment we found each
other in that church.

I remember that July:
me standing before you,
making a poem turn hymnal,
every ancestor in the room
pushing us closer to each other.

It's almost been a year, and
on the days I can't find Faith,
I cup your face into my palms
and this is the closest I can

get to Spirit. We both practice
a religion that knows no bounds
to this life, meaning our love
knows no limits here.

You, my comrade,
the best friend I merely
imagined as a child,
the only one who gets it.

Our love is the metro line from
downtown to Santa Monica
being our jungle gym.
It is binge-watching
Chopped and *Catfish*
in your family's living room.
It is the organizing we pour
ourselves into. It is the community
that receives us.

You, my shelter every time.

My real childhood home.

Our love is Sundays,
fried shrimp and cake
from Southern Girl in
Leimert Park with drum circles
entrancing us in front of the fountain.

It's every elderly person we walk by saying,
"Now, that's love . . . Don't you dare lose one another."
You have been my lighthouse
since I first came into this world—
every moment has led me to the one
I washed upon the shore of you.

You.
There is not much I can say
to give our love justice
so instead
I write these poems
or sing you Lauryn Hill off-key,
give you a book to read,
hold your hand wherever we go.
Because God,
I don't want to lose this moment or you.
And if love knows no limits,
you are the only type of love
that makes me wish my body
won't ever fail me again –

that we won't ever have
to go back to your cot
next to my hospital bed,
angry at all the times we avoided
something being so wrong
that I almost died.

Honey,
I keep thinking of last night
when I said I was sad because
I don't know why I am here. But
remember when you asked me
to marry you in the apartment?
And I thought it was a joke
because we had been dating for
two weeks but I blushed and
said yes anyway. Somehow
I knew I wanted to be the one
to hold your future and mine
in our shared engagement rings.
The night you got down on one knee,
we cried coming home from the beach
because how could something
like this happen to kids like us?

So, love,
I am counting down the days
until I can have that future
and all our morning musings turn reality,
and our reality becomes the most sacred truth:
a small house, you chasing after our pets
in a forest-filled backyard. Me, sipping coffee
and writing yet another one of these poems.
And we will forget about April of that year.
And the cancer by then will be so small.

You, the gatekeeper to the
estate of my heart will say
the leukemia has forgotten
how to fight, then make
a *Pootie Tang* joke about
cancer's weak ass, then
flip on Dead Prez.

And yes,
ain't nothing ever promised to us
but I choose to be a promise to you
and you choose to have Faith in me.
And the church will always bellow an amen to that,
our love always the sweetest hallelujah.

A Brief Autobiographical Moment
in My Cancer Support Group

Prompt: connection to and with people lies at the heart of healing

When I was barely five, I told a man yee-hawing
in an elevator at the Beverly Center to shut up.
Explained to my mother she knew nothing about
raising children; therefore, I did not have to listen.

I was observant enough to make a man
unable to recognize his own skin.
Make anyone doubt themselves.
I didn't believe things should be
the way they are out of formality.

When I was eight, my mom grabbed my hair.
Flung my head back and forth out of anger.
I didn't name it Betrayal, just Loss of Innocence.

When I was thirteen, my grandmother died.
Five years later—her sister did too,
and I haven't forgiven God since.

In high school, older boys at summer camp
fetishized me. Thought Black girls
were "fast and easy"—meant to be hidden.
Back then, I was my mother's rib,

couldn't go anywhere she was not.
Solace became a razor blade,
a sip of alcohol,
smoking my first cigarette
in a New York City subway.

After I dropped out of college,
sex was not sex. I said: rape.
My mother said: prove it,
and I never mentioned the
other times after.
Assault left my vocabulary.

Got one too many tattoos one year
and my father said leave,
my mother agreed.

Blood runs thin at home.

The doctors think it took around
three to four years for the cancer
to spiral out like my mental health.

I trace that to my mother disowning me.
Like her body wasn't a house to my organs first.

When I met Ivie,
she was the only one
that said Friend

and meant it,
said love
and I believed it.

Sometimes I recall the ways people have lied to me.
I spent years sick without knowing.
Heard the empty *"You look okay to me."*
But nothing was okay, and that too is a betrayal.

Vows people made,
pleading, *"If Walela could just live, then ..."*
And how many Hail Marys have gone forgotten since?
And that is a betrayal of sorts as well.

I don't trust most people.
The elders in my family would say it is a past life speaking.
But I've given up my body and everything that comes
with it to an unforgiving-ass world.
I am allegedly not worthy of patience.
Must I perform a miracle with ten daggers in my back?
Make communion out of nothing?
A baptism to initiate the easing into cognitive dissonance?

It is lonely to know nobody holds me like I hold myself.
To know it is but my breath that morning depends on.
And that's when Doubt is given my reflection.
A new name. And this is when I'm most honest.

Therefore, most vulnerable. This is the part I hate.
That I let nobody see. The part where I question
everyone who has passed on or those who have
passed me by in this life: *"But why didn't you stay?"*

A tenderness only reserved for myself,
where no one, not even me,
can hurt myself.
What is a child
with no mother,
no father,
but they are both
still living?
Does that make
me a ghost, too?
—*The Haunting*

Phantom Pain

Each being in my family
has made their wrists crack
from rotating and massaging
their lower backs.
Using scented balm, steroids,
gritted teeth, and CBD to cast
out the throbbing Morse code:
What's been done is done.
It don't matter if we are half collapsed
over the sink, folding laundry,
or seasoning tonight's dinner on a skillet.
The muscles squeeze our lumbar spines.
Their reasons for stiffening vary,
but every single one
is a courtesy warning, I suppose.
Incoming recollections manifest
as the dark brown, freckled scar
on my lower back, a peephole
designed for an aching inheritance.

Tracing Roots of a Family Tree

I don't really know anybody other than a great-grandparent or two before my diagnosis in 2017. December and tinfoil-wrapped palm trees with red bows adorn the streets. I sip on coffee with journal entries sprawled out before me of places to remember, names to look into, possible misspellings. I am trying to find my people. I stare at photos of censuses. Excitedly look up the listed address of where they lived. What was once there is now replaced by something new. More industrial. I longingly look at the land, wishing to plunge my hand into the dirt, because maybe that will tell me something a picture can't. Another riddle answered.

I hold on to death certificates. A computer screen leaves me mystified because death certificates are always how I learn who mothered the ancestor that died. Only as a trail of bodies in the ground do I learn my origins, and ain't that something worth mourning for an eternity?

I discover draft cards for imperialist wars and learn how tall some of the men in my family were, their ages, if they were disabled: a drive-by interview of sorts. I clutch on to a memory living inside of a battered camel-colored square with obsidian cursive handwriting. I save marriage certificates, government papers, "find a grave" indexes. I crawl up my family tree, swing down branches, searching for more, and yet there is nothing.

I start tracing far enough back for one part of my line until I amble into a crisp white wallpapered room: the "master," the "owner" Mathews is the only cursive. We don't have names worth documenting. We are numbers. On a slave schedule. Tracked and traded as human livestock. Other ancestors intentionally hid themselves from being found for righteous reasons I will never know. Point is, I don't find freedom anywhere. Mostly conjectures. Violence cycles as it reinvents itself, coinciding with the ways slavery has reinvented itself, and scarring so much that the root is obstructed from sight.

I know, like most Black families, nobody wants to talk about the horror. Heard stories about elders saying better to forget, to tuck it away. The need to look forward so the past can stretch behind us farther and farther while miles of promise and potential can sprawl out ahead of us. To my family, to look forward is to be hopeful that there is a better future, maybe not for their generation, but maybe the next one. And the next one after that. The mighty prayer that time can hopefully erase the horrific theft of an entire people.

If Ernie Barnes's *A Walk in Faith* Portrait Could Walk Out the Frame

In Ivie's attic, I meet an ancestor for the first time without knowing it. A small altar transfigured into an oak-ridged door. Her spirit finds the skeleton key and steps into the mortal world. My body, unwillingly motionless, turned on its right side. I cannot see her, but I hear her. An older woman putzing around a creaky attic. Picking up dirty clothes, even Ivie's underwear, off the dirty baby-blue carpet, questioning why they were on the ground to begin with. I am soundless. No answer. Footsteps scuff toward the twin bed. Ivie snoring. My neck coiled forcefully in place like the Bent-Neck Lady. A cerulean dress fills my dilated pupils. The clock fossilizes. At breakfast, I read about a fourth great-aunt: Susan. The record is transcribed to the tempo she spoke in. Born in 1856. Enslaved until Emancipation. Reconstruction is her mom and dad leaving. Susan was born and raised in Jasper and lived at Magnolia Springs. I skim. Too early in the day to read and the blotchy parts require too much of me. I scan until midway through the document. Her vocal chiming clear and magnified:

> *"I marry when Is fourteen and*
> *de Rev. George Hammonds,*
> *he perform de ceremony.*
>
> *We marry*
> *quiet at home*
> *and I wore*
> *blue dress."*

U.S., Interviews with Formerly Enslaved People, 1936–1938
Magnolia Springs, Freedom Colonies, The Texas Freedom Colony Project

Portrait of Remembrance

In photographs of the women in my family,
white flowers attach to hair clips and
extravagant Sunday church hats.
Shoulders pushed back, their faces
up close, in focus with lips curved
upward, hiding a sinister secret.
The flowers, magnolias, waft in
the air with hints of lynchings
and torched-down livelihoods.
Billie Holiday sang about it.
Strange fruit indeed.
We don't got the same scent
after fleeing, I mean migrating.
Los Angeles ain't Jasper,
so when the women in my family die,
their invisible heavenly bodies drift
to Magnolia Springs. I stay in a small
church in South Central. Collect petals
off their caskets. Signifying the impermanence
of home and the permanence of terror.

jasper, tx:

Each year,
jasper county offers
free shuttle rides
to the Butterfly Festival.
Monarch butterflies
migrate through the county.
Behold, a swarm of brilliant
orange insects. Their safe passage
marveled at by white people.

In jasper, safe passage
is denied for Black folks.
A free ride is never free.
Three white supremacists
drunk on amerikkkan ideals
grind a truck against asphalt.
Dragged Black man
James Byrd "for free"
across three miles
to meet a severing.

In jasper,
Black means locust.
The racists, red-faced,
proclaim the great migration
was supposed to mean exodus.

In 1998, the leftover Black population
are considered a swarm of vermin.
Behold, when the middle passage
isn't enough for settlers, the roads
will repave in streams of blood-soaked
cowrie shells.* The odor
of decomposing Black corpses
will suffice instead.

Lose Your Mother by Saidiya Hartman

I've Always Wanted a Big Family

Ivie has an enormous family compared to my own. Aunties and uncles and cousins and grandparents who are still living file in for any occasion that Ivie's mother decides is worth cleaning the house over: holidays, birthdays, random weekends. Wakes up and does that thing Black mamas do: "Lord, this house gotta get done, y'all!" I split chores with Ivie and her twin. We vigorously sweep the den's hardwood floor full of lint, dust, spare paper, caps to pens that have gone missing, and mesh them into piles to take out with the trash. We make the dirtiness "more presentable." Stacking piles out of the books we've been reading there late at night like: Assata's autobiography or *Feminist Theory* by bell hooks or *Settlers* by J. Sakai. The den is farthest from the front door, but it is where the TV is; therefore, the most important room for guests who will eventually retire in there to watch *Atlanta* or whatever football game is on between two teams I don't know anything about.

The next important place: the dining room because that's where everybody is going to bring the dish they made and Ivie's mother needs space to cook. Ivie scrubs at saucepans coated in soyaki from a stir-fry Ivie's mom made days ago. Ivie immerses her long arms into a sink that's too small for a house this big but makes do with one sponge and some Dawn liquid soap. Ivie's mom hops around the kitchen in her pajamas making biscuits, macaroni and cheese, and her famous delicately sweet strawberry-yogurt cake. One time, when the family came over last, I was told the story that Ivie cried at her cousin's birthday party at around eight years old because the baked cake was too dry for her liking. I busted up laughing alongside everyone around me. "It's too dry," she imitates as a mournful whine that never fails to sound ridiculous yet adorably very much like Ivie.

The living room is more of a temporary seating area by the door, with African art pieces hanging on the wall and a mantel of family photographs: Ivie and her twin as toddlers, their younger sister as a baby, the cousins' yearbook photos framed. It's an homage I am not used to seeing. Everyone shuffles in, and nearly each time, I'm introduced to someone new. I like Ivie's family. There's always someone for the kids to play with, there's always a conversation to hop into or observe, a family game to play, and despite being Ivie's fiancée, I know I am not their family in the same way everyone else is in the room to one another. Loyal to one another no matter who is wrong or right: family is blood, and blood comes above all else. I want to mean that to somebody, but most of my extended family is up north or in Texas still—and not just anywhere in Texas: the deep country. Being in the middle of a huge family reminds me what being a continent away from home feels like. I often cannot stay long these days. I get dressed after cleaning, say hello, eat some food, listen to a few stories, then run upstairs to the attic. To my altar. And pray for more ancestors to step through the door.

Degnan Blvd

Houses on Degnan Blvd are split by massive trees separating
    the sides of the road.
Ivie's home is off Crenshaw and King, a little ways past the
    Krispy Kreme and
a right on Degnan. Drive down 'til you get close to Stocker, 2017,
the height of gentrification is starting to sow its reaping.
Degnan is the only house without a green lawn to accompany
the red-brick cobblestoned walkway. Vines cover chipped
    white paint at the entrance.
The house always looks as if someone is moving in or out.
    Piles of boxes,
books, paper, furniture, or other supplies to aid Etsy
    get-rich-quick schemes by Ivie's mom.
Nothing is ever fully clean except on Mother's Day—we pool
    money for mostly me
to pay for a top-down scrubbing. No one can account for the
    busted basketball frame
in the back, leaves piling inside the unheated pool, or Ivie's
    experiment dump truck
to play mechanic on. There is always junk. Everywhere.
A Russian doll with unending rivers of mess.

A Christmas Baptism into Hell aka The Honeymoon Phase Is Unexpectedly Over for Unforeseen Reasons

There is no evidence that this day would come and create a prism of how to perceive you, me, and us. Lovers have snapped at me before, but I never anticipated your fist punching through a wall at random. No place to set down your frustration with me, my cancer, and all the space it takes up. Like dry ice to warm water, cancer done bubbled the patience out of you. Pushed misdirected sorrow into an empty space.

Mad at me for being sad about broken promises of "the best Christmas ever" and mentions of selling your expensive record collection because you were getting something "So Special" for your "pookie" for making it through this cancer thing. This morning I gingerly opened a cardboard Dr. Martens box filled with IOUs written the night before in Sharpie.

In the attic, away from everyone, my disappointed expectations make a calm climb up the stairs. We spent months reminding each other of how special holidays are, and what I am trying to say is that I wanted to feel special. I do not know what I said. I only know it was the wrong thing.

Your mouth snarled into accusations of me being "ungrateful." Yelled about your part-time job with no mention of the bills you do not pay—your family does that for you. This was the first time your pupils dilated so large I thought you had to be possessed. On the hot-pink comforter covering our bed, I became a small cave where my words retreated and tears sprayed out.

You looked on without apology for a blink, then fell to the ground crying. Squirming and wailing, your pain so much worse than mine. I could set mine down. Pressed my eyes together like my tears had to be wrung out of a damp towel. Pushed my jar of qualms under the bed. Glided to the ground beside you, rubbed your back, cooing, *"It's okay, it's okay,"* regretting the way my feelings always needed to be expressed.

"All Alone on Christmas" — Darlene Love

After helping Ivie through her breakdown,
I rushed down the spiraling staircase.
Discovered an empty home downstairs.
Looked out the kitchen window
and saw she'd tied my pen
to the back of her family's car.

They all zoomed off,
then I relapsed.
Ate like a ravenous lion.
Cut myself repeatedly 'til my hands
turned raspberry. Binged on a tub of pasta,
watched those ABC Family Claymation movies, crying.
Worked out to PopSugar videos on YouTube.
Strained my muscles to compensate for the guilt relapse.

This is not my first Christmas alone.
But it's my first one alone and in love.
I know the absence of family.
I wasn't prepared for the possibility
that there may be an absence of love here.
Because that's impossible.
She slipped up; I know her.
She's overwhelmed. We're young;
it happens. Mistakes happen.

I can't shake how my mind's eye
wandered when I saw letters flying
out the trunk of her mom's car.
All those words, unsaid,
littering the street.
My poems held hostage
like the baggage
under Ivie's bed.
Like the drywall
to her fist.

Synonym for Gaslighting

Unflinching.
Her mouth
makes space
for the words
to grow in size.
She debates
whether or not
to hold on to
the truth,
but the lies
have already
formed
in the tiny spaces
between her teeth.
Unblinking,
with phrases
intentionally
overemphasized.
She pretends
to be
something
she is not.
Gifting me
bouquets of red
carnations,

a letter
apologizing,
our song:
"For the Love of You"
spins on vinyl.
She invites me
to dance.
Takes off
my ring.
Gets down
on one knee.
Re-proposing.
Accusing my brain
of misremembering.

Work, Work, Work, Work, Work, or Whatever Rihanna Said

The hole in the wall
has stayed open,
staring at me
ever since the incident.
My sadness was breathing
too hot on Ivie's neck.
The pen is a weapon
of self-defense, though.
I take out my journal,
document a soon-to-be bygone
followed with a:
Do everything you can
to never depend on anybody again.
Nobody cares about you
as much as you care about you.
I pull up to the neighborhood holistic shop.
Get hired so the forty-hour weeks will
work the ungratefulness right outta me,
so Ivie cannot draw disparaging remarks
as weapons of invalidation ever again.

The Bad Black Cancer Patient Who Leapt Through Time

(inspired by *The Girl Who Leapt Through Time*)

I relapse with a knife while staring in Ivie's full-length mirror.
I take to my left thigh. Become a fascinated carpenter.
My leg, a leaking wildfire. Make it so I got two heartbeats,
but at least I don't gotta confront myself.

Avoid my reflection—Me at twenty-three years old.
Forced to revisit—Me at twelve years old.
We both got the same bulb of anger.
We both wanna catch a deep breath.
Catch the euphoria, then methodically:
disinfect, bandage, hide.
Practice the faux smile we learned as a child.
I lie to my own face, meaning I lie to my ancestors,
the altar, famished and dirty.
I drop the knife back on top of it.
There's no hello from me,
no offering made,
the water long evaporated.

Have you no shame, child?
Return to the water—

I ignore them.
Walk downstairs,
kiss Ivie so that
Everything is okay
becomes
Nothing ever happened.

"Yeah, some guy was talking about
how he just hopes she dies sometimes.
And I was like, thank God I don't feel
that way about you. It scared me,"
Ivie blurts out, laughing in between
sips of a Frappuccino at The Coffee
Bean & Tea Leaf a block away
from the train station home.
Our pit stop after separate
support group meetings:
one for the patient,
one for the caregiver.

In Santa Monica,
she declares,
"I don't want to go back,
I couldn't relate to
what they were saying,
I could never see myself going that far.
It actually made me relieved we aren't like that."

I chew on my purple straw without glancing up.
I don't underestimate the unpredictable.
I pause, slowly relay, *"You should really*
talk with your family about finding a therapist

. . . because this shit"—I motion everywhere,
indicating cancer's omnipotence—
"this shit is gonna fuck you up."
—The Coffee Bean & Tea Leaf's
   Secret Menu Item Is Avoidance

Two Black People with Medi-Cal Walk into a Bar

Stevie is on Medi-Cal too.
Did not receive the instruction manual either.
We use obscure humor and hyperspecific jokes
that only if you were Black, disabled, and
on some of the government's worst insurance
then you could hop in on. Use laughter to cope
with the realization: It don't matter how sick you are,
you'll be blamed for your own symptoms.
Showing up early for appointments won't change
that you'll be in the waiting room for over two hours.
Don't show up five minutes late, though
—you will get penalized.
When a system barricades care solely for the worthy
and we don't make the list—the rest of us are led
out to pasture, wandering a political field:
our own body left to slaughter itself
on the government's behalf.

"is it me, am i the problem?"

Instagram got influencers for makeup
but no Black cancer patients to look up to.

We don't show up in TV, movies,
on YouTube, or hosting podcasts.
We don't got stories.
Nothing that can be passed down.

If I'm my big ole age and can't listen
to anyone who has fictionally survived
cancer or find Black people who haven't
died from cancer, then what does that say
about our odds in reality?

How is there no
documentation of this?
What did we do that was
so wrong for society to be
our dismayed mother letting
us go this unaccounted for?

We Can't Buy a Cure, but We Can Sure Try

Just because I work in a holistic health store
doesn't mean downing every supplement is
going to take away the leukemia.
But it won't prevent me from trying.

I knock back a handful of echinacea,
gulp on alkaline water, swig tablespoons
of black seed oil, ingest CKLS pills at my register.
Day in, day out, during my forty-hour workweek,
Black people come in asking, "Do you have anything
that can help with [insert disability], [insert chronic illness]."

Western medicine claims there ain't nothing
out there meant to save us negroes.
We go to a shop like the one I work at and
attempt to attribute our health to a personal failing.
Because. If we failed, then we can fix ourselves.

We refute our bodies not being to "standard."
I am no different than my customers,
I am no naturopath,
but experimentation is easier on the psyche than
a white-collar doctor who is more invested in
debating my Black bleak reality than being,
I don't know . . . a medical professional.

If we can eradicate what the doctors claim
as indiscernible, our bodies can DIY-project
themselves into a one-size-fits-all solution.
Reliance, then, is no longer within the system
but with ourselves inside this tiny crowded store.
I am no different than the women who ask for
the shop's fibroid cleanse in hushed tones.
Or the laborers who ask what aisle has the drink
that clears out a cold overnight cuz none of us
can afford to miss a day's worth of pay.
I restock aisles packed with bottles holding
our agency and ring up my own convictions:
I can cure myself with an employee discount.

Burdensome Horrors

The olive oil cleanse advertised at my job sent me to the ER.
Apparently, no human body should consume that much
    oil in one sitting.
This isn't my first trip back to the ER. It's a routine by now.
The other month Chick-fil-A sent me in at 10:30 p.m.
Colds from counting strangers' money at my job WWE–wrestle
with my immune system, and I am sick for blurs of
    time with infections
cropping up. For the theme of selling health, my job doesn't seem
to clean anywhere. Layered grime on the ceilings or corners
    of the store.
I eat a menu item from the adjacent restaurant, and my liver
washes itself the color of sunflowers. An African
    nurse practitioner
eyes the chart I clutch to my side to relieve the stabbing pain,
"You're on this oral chemo?" I grimace a yes.
"You got diagnosed with cancer when?"
"It hasn't been a year yet."
She looks at me as if she watched
a horror movie character walk into a trap.
The trap: an unsanitary job with the public
will get you sicker than sick when you already sick.
"Your immune system doesn't work like everybody else's,
why are you working here?"

"Because my partner is in school, and I don't have a degree."

"But you're sick, with cancer. You can't work like this."

My jaw prevents the pop scare of my thoughts:

I have to so no one will be mad at me for being a burden.

The Isle of Misfit Toys

I'm not a good worker by Capitalism's standards.
Boss believes money is leaking out the register
because I don't move faster than fast.
I been working for a few months now.
Five a.m. restocks on Wednesdays.
Men call me sexy, then become disgusted
when they find out about the cancer.
Customer service is delivering a fantasy
even in a hole-in-the-wall store.
Snap-snap and shapeshift into whatever
the person who got the credit card or
wad of cash in their pocket wants.
My pelvic bone bangs on my lower back
from the biopsies I keep having to do off the clock.
This job violates about every other health code
and labor law, but California is an at-will state,
so I'm not surprised on Wednesday when
I am laid off without explanation.
Remember what I said about silence earlier?
It can get loud with the last conversations we had.
A worker asking for—a stool at my register.
Accommodations = a worker who knows
their rights will infect the other workers
to believe they got rights too.

Even by "holistic health standards,"
I am a defunct worker with phantom pain
lacerating keyholes into my lumbar spine.
My last check,
a passport to the Isle of Misfit Toys.

But You Don't Look Sick

You can't
be sick
You don't
look it
Look
disabled
I mean
I don't
know
what sick
or disabled
looks like
Idk what
a compromised
immune system
is supposed
to look like
but, like,
Where
the gaunt
face at?
Your hair
ain't lost
somewhere
Sometimes,
you laugh

You wear
makeup
and it don't
look like
a mortician's
handiwork
You ain't
like patients
in those
nonprofit
commercials
You don't
look like
a white,
bald woman
dying
to induce
pity donations
I'm not used
to sick people
still lookin'
like life
is finding
a way
through
their face
I'm so
miserable
I cannot
admit

that
someone
I believe
to be
effortlessly
suffering
actually
enrages me

My Great-Uncle Claudius Will Never Be Included in Who *Moulin Rouge!* Was About

Thank you, Susan Sontag

Consumption is not desire, lust,
imagination, or a message
of the angels descending.
Ask my grandaddy's brother.
He would agree.

Tuberculosis, also once called consumption,
was a disease only given from the Lord on high
to white aristocrats or artists. For anyone darker,
such as . . . Black, TB was the mark of Cain on the lungs.

My great-uncle Claudius was seventeen when he contracted it.
Casts on an X-ray, the cough, a subsequent hospitalization.
He was a child, with working parents in Kerrville, Texas.
In Kerrville, there was never a good time to be sick.
There was not a *Moulin Rouge!* musical sequence
    after the diagnosis.
No twenty-string quartet or dancers from Cirque du Soleil
or people eagerly waiting at his bedside for whatever deity
to speak through him.

I don't know what his December in the hospital was like.
The dead won't tell you those things.
Don't wanna scare you away with going to the other side.

It becomes easy to question religion when a teenager
dies on Christmas at 11:20 p.m. at 17 years, 5 months,
    and 13 days old.
And don't you dare say he was too good for this world
or that he was "being called home" because he did
all that he was supposed to do in this world.

Did Claudius get to do *all* of what he really wanted to do?
For a disease so obsessed with the blushes of consuming life
"to the fullest," so much so, it breaks outta you like a night
sweat and makes you fall in love so you won't die miserably.
Did Claudius get to fall in love? Did anyone tell him he was loved.
In fact. He was loved so much so he would not be forgotten.
He did not have the luxury of being sick and worthy.
History proving those two will never exist at the same time
    for Black folk.

I Find Out How My Great-Grandmother Died

Pearl,
I've been silent since it all.
I don't know where
sound goes in stillness.
My body stitched itself closed.
Cancer treatment has made it
to where I have not menstruated.
Before the diagnosis, I would flush
a barricade of quarter-sized clots.
I am told the cancer will "stagnate"
my reproductive organs.
I consider this your protection.
Two out of your three children lived
—my grandaddy being one, Aunt Billie
the other, but Uncle Claudius died.
Rumor has it, Another was aborted.
Pro-lifers will claim your punishment
was a pelvic abscess. Dying alone
as an unread manifesto.
I imagine all my unshed blood
writes the lyrics. The bleeding,
a poem left behind on a tiled
hospital room floor reading:
I can only bear the weight
of birthing myself as legacy.

Enemy of the State

Dedicated in loving memory of Dr. Mutulu Shakur (1950–2023):
freedom fighter, leukemia warrior, and community health advocate

Black people are not people.
We are unseen ideas.

Cancer is not for the human.
It, too, is an idea.
Cancer did not benefit
from its cousin tuberculosis.
With diagnosis being
an ascension
to enlightenment.

No, the symptoms
were never made
into an aspiration.

Cancer went from illness to metaphor
for the very worst things. Writers too lazy
to make any other parallels about invisible
forces of evil round up cancer as tribute.
Society writes diatribes, weaponizing cancer
to awaken the imagination—political orientation
does not matter. Cancer was and still is the all-
encompassing vehicle for whatever is wicked,
immoral, or corrupt.

Cancer, an "unexplainable," "mean-spirited"
phenomenon. Ravishes anyone who will host it.
To host it is to host an enemy of the state,
an enemy to the people, a barrier to freedom.

Cancer is a trained sniper to not only its host
but to everyone surrounding the host.

Cancer is: Us vs. It.
As a patient,
cancer is
You vs. It
but also
The World vs. It.

"The War on Cancer" is fine and well.
But it, the cancer, lives inside you.

By default, you are now an opposing force
to the good of humanity.

A therapist at my cancer support center
asks me to draw what my leukemia looks like,
and Black Crayola forges a web of tentacles.

Riddle:
If a Black person is an idea
and cancer is an idea,
then will the illness ever be real?
Will the person ever have existed?

If you have so many ideas and
hardly any grounded in reality,
do the ideas have their own stories too?

Thinking:
To be Black is to be a non-thing,
a nothing, not human, barely animal.
They will accuse you of letting an angel
draw its long fingernail against your neck
to drain your mortality and morality.
Bad ideas like Black people and cancer
are not meant to coexist. Must be cut out,
taken into the woods, and put down.
Removed as a smudge on the windows
of humanity or experimented on as an idea
that gives way to an idea that gives way
to an idea and so on.

Answer:
The Black cancer patient is a mythical fascination.
A playground for the author's and reader's perception.
Only as real and tangible as our will allows them to be.

Delusions of Prophecies

We been stolen over and over.
So. Traditions are lost. Or. They Morph.
And the ways of knowing change into denial.

The women in my family have dreams,
will write, will draw, will pull the cards,
will absentmindedly say something
and it comes true.
The women in my family are seers.
In this world, premonitions are reserved for:
The Crazy, The Insane, The *chillleee*
that's enough to get you put in the loony bin.
Knowing your ancestry is an arrowhead spear.
You a danger to self and others.
Yet I'm supposed to believe
we must be "blessed"
by white evangelical pastors
who got a "personal connection" with God?
Their "prophecies" are lies.
A white man's religion will never
dictate what is or is not righteous for me.
The God for white people
ain't the same
as my grandmother's God
or her mother's God.

There is a commitment
to have us unbecome ourselves.

Under colonialism's nasty snarl,
at a square altar, I am finding my way back.
Meditating with spirits spinning around the room.
Dear God,
when are you gonna tell them
the truth, or shall I?

"One of the most painful things about being a human being, in my opinion, is when you feel like you're not of use to anyone and you have nothing to give. It's heartbreaking. And a lot of people who are sick feel that way because just taking care of themselves takes up so much of their time."

—*Claire Wineland*

two Black Medi-Cal patients walk
into the county building

and run through the government,
rings of fire to be considered
for financial aid: general relief,
food stamps, disability.
The county building ain't
no different than a Medi-Cal
doctor's office.
The overstimulation of noise:
folks haggling over cell phones
sold out front, babies crying,
blurts of frustration,
and the occasional last name
called out for one out of the
fifty waiting to be interviewed.
The interview is synonym for:
Are you really outta money?
The answer is yes.
With a job? yes.
Without a job? yes.
Counterquestion:
You ever heard of the cost of living?
Right . . .
Run me that check.

The county building is the gauntlet.

I sit across the table from a non-Black person.
A white-passing Latinx woman reviews my paperwork.
I bounce my knee, looking at the clock, then her.
The clock, then her. I'm about *this close*
to handing her a magnifying glass since
she knows that I know the long pause
is her search for discrepancies.

Lets out a triumphant,
"oh nooo"
Holy hell,
I prefer straight-up apathy over this insincerity.
"You forgot the doctor's note."

Nobody told me about a doctor's note
the last time I was here. For four hours.
Ain't the insurance plan I been assigned to
an LA County program? Don't y'all got
a way of talking—like . . . on a phone?
I can't get ahold of anybody by myself,
have left more voicemails on the phones
of doctors, social workers, and help lines
than all my ex-lovers combined.

No answer.

I am "boo-hoo it's a sob story #35"
of the day and Stevie is #43.
We are but numbers on a piece of paper.
Ain't no welfare queens or people
tryna "cheat the system" anywhere.
Everyone is pleading a case:
Survival—to a jury of one:
a relentlessly cruel government.

i don't care if he "saved" my life, after this i'm switching oncologists

All these poor people
come into my office
and ask for a letter.
They all milk the system
instead of going to work.

I would slap him into next year
but Woosah it out, I guess

I close my purple folder:
a briefcase containing the evidence,
proof, of what the county building is requesting.

Pierce through his classism,
"these poor people need help,"
reminding him:
a doctor not in service
to the people
is in service to his ego,
the morgue,
and a checkbook.

The World Don't Care If You're Broke, Everything Comes at a Cost

Broken promises in an engagement are illegal,
or so I think. Maybe I'm tryna say
I don't believe in compromise on my own behalf.
I play major chords on a piano, Ivie plays the minor,
and it's all black-and-white logic up in here.
I ain't tryna lose our sheet music in the grim alleyway
of curveballs—like layoffs without unemployment,
and the Benjamins still gotta find a way into my bank account.
Ivie deserves more than my life's unpredictability.
I let her keep playin' on the bench of our imaginary musical.
It's not an intermission; it's a swift adjustment.
A new hustle. An old concept:
Ask for help from strangers, except on the internet:

                           [insert paylinks here]

Luck Be a Roll-a-Dice When You a Nigga:

For Teighlor, founder of Black Disability Collective

Oftentimes I am asked
if I feel lucky to still be alive
To which I say,
If my cancer didn't kill me,
something else would have
If a bullet from a Nazi,
I mean,
white supremacist,
I mean, a cop's gun
didn't lodge itself
into my spine
Trust, the system
would still have found
a way to kill me
And if repression
wouldn't have done it,
I know it would have
been something else

I think of the places
I lived before the hospital
How I could name three liquor stores
within a mile radius but only one grocery store
My stomach would often be a hungry vulture

I think of how I've watched people
make money a false altar
—This country, a false idol
What kind of god
needs my knees broken
to show respect?

I think back to before the hospital again
and how I didn't go to a doctor for years
because I knew one wouldn't see me
Let my uninsured veins inflate
with white blood cells,
believing anything,
including a grave,
was better than medical debt

When I was finally hospitalized,
a nurse told me if I waited a second longer,
my organs would've started failing
Funny how it took two clinics turning
me away before I got the care I needed
Heard a nurse whisper I must be on drugs
—so yeah, If the cancer didn't kill me,
If the police don't kill me, the State
will make it so my own DNA would

Doctor explained my bone marrow
was filled to the brim with cancer cells
and that it was all siphoning into my bloodstream
It became a new type of poison and now

I swallow a poison twice a day that Big Pharma
invests in because keeping me alive on this
oral chemo for as long as possible is contingent
on how fat of a check is cut to them
—Fuck the side effects,
the millions of dollars misappropriated
to "cure cancer." With nonprofits
it's the profit that counts

It's like the stock value rises
the closer I get to dying,
to lookin' casket-sharp
It's like if I ain't worth being abused
by capitalism, I become yet another
sad "tragedy." Nah, I don't feel so lucky
to be alive when all my time is borrowed
Just like every other Black person
But I guess that's the best I can expect
when all my ancestors were "borrowed" here
Their backs breaking carrying this damn country
while watching our kin sink into the soil.
Amerikkka is one thirsty child
And he stay feeding on our blood

What's luck
when you always hear him calling?
What's luck
when a diagnosis don't make ableism disappear?
Don't make the fight or flight pause?
It's like I gotta pay to be alive

& *anything* I need is a toll
& all this living I'm doin'
is really me tryna escape
what would kill me
I won't ever know peace
for I was never made to—
Every part of life is a war
so know if I die,
then it's a murder.
Take me in an urn,
throw my ashes at the State,
and tell that
mothafucka to burn

In this dream,

the cancer throws
me back in the hospital.
The doctors say again,
"There's nothing more we can do."
Except this time, they mean it.
This time, the cancer mutates.
And no one is shocked.
In this dream,
everyone tells me like the last time,
"Nothing is wrong."
But everything is wrong.
This time, like the last,
there are no symptoms.
This time, unlike the last,
my body just lets me go.
This time, I'm hollow
with baby's breath,
and I can't do this anymore.
My grandma hugs me.
Soothingly smiles:
"Baby, it's okay.
You said the same to me,
and that's what let me
let go of myself."
April 1, 2007 = April Fool's Day
but also Palm Sunday, 2007.

An airplane from
JFK to LAX eclipses
the clouds—
my grandma's spirit
ascends outside my
Virgin America window.
In this dream, the cancer
is my grandma, her sister
& my grandaddy.
And I want it (them)
to take me wholly.
My eulogy,
an empty room.

I Go Searching for My Mother in the Wrong People

I am looking for anyone to claim me as their child at the
    lost and found.
Longing is a vice, and Ivie's mother sees it in me before I do.
She lures me in with promises of healing and rest
because, for "God's sake," I have cancer
and I am the eldest daughter she always wanted.
We sit over morning coffee, holding oversized ceramic mugs.
She in a robe and me in sweatpants, our hair completely
    out of place.
We trade factoids from our ancestry records—after all,
my family is her family now. There's a lot I do not know.
Ivie's mother seems to have tranquilizers ready with oxblood
    serums of truth and my secrets. Mentions moments I could've
    sworn I only told Ivie. Offers her unsolicited maternal insight.
Offers help. With g'ttin' back into college. Nudges at me to
    figure out how to try
and file for disability, again, for the third time, but my social
    worker's number keeps changing.

Ivie's mother speaks highly of a social worker friend,
mentions she'll do a skill trade with the lady so I can get
that government help finally. Makes a joke out the side of her neck
about how Ivie and I should have babies. *"The government
    pays good for those."*
My chemo sits on the table with a *"Walela's body is
    out of service"* sign.

In sync with sunrise, she suggests I be nicer, less intense.

I guess I am too similar to my mother.

I just need to be more . . . understanding, out here holding people

to impossible standards like: communication and honesty.

After enough hours and mornings, I listen and believe her.

Invite her to come with me to an oncology appointment.

She shows up to one. Forgets about the others. This

    ain't new terrain.

But she's instilled enough faith that I keep faith out of patience.

The sun creeps over the horizon, and I cannot stop compulsively

    searching for a mother.

Words always sound better on paper or in passing. However,

    Action deems who and what

is worth the time. Return me back to the lost and found

    of hypervigilance.

Ivie's mom already missed the memo: false promises

    come back around

—I'm waiting to get picked up elsewhere.

Neutrality Is Not Peaceful

I stop journaling about Ivie's mom
and decide to say out loud:
"your mom be doin' some weirdo
shit like . . ." [read poem above]
Ivie snaps. Her mom is off-limits from critique.
Supposedly. It is because she feels an allegiance
to the both of us. I just need to "calm down"
and keep journaling my "issues" to myself.
Without hesitancy, I zip up my backpack
of qualms. Drop it off at My Brain's:
No One Cares, Stop Whining Department
& wander into the Neutrality Aisle instead.

It's My Party and I Can't Cry If I Want To

Another rotation around the sun.
Twenty-four.
Ivie's mom smiles at the bottom of the staircase.
I can read her well enough to tell the difference
between her smiles—with this one,
she 'bout to ask me for something.
She closes her arms around my torso for a hug.
I do not like being touched but let her squeeze tight
because this is my "new mom." And like many mothers,
she attempts to make me into something in her image.
I am defiant. Today, though, she mistakenly assumes otherwise,
says, *"I can call you [insert dead name] today, right?*
Your mom gave you that name for a reason."
My no is not enough,
and I am quickly learning consent is but
a concept to the academic adults of this family,
the "professors" of our new enlightened generation.
"Please, please, please, for me,
it's your birthday, let me call you
[insert dead name]."
Like I owe her the gift of transphobia.

The Assumptions

You are a woman.

You have a boyfriend.

You are heterosexual.

You answer to [insert dead name].

You go by she/her.

You are not who you say you are.

You are who we believe you are.

We don't keep up with the times.

Because we are only here for medicine.

We don't care about your gender.

We care about your vagina.

And your vagina makes you a woman.

We don't care about your girlfriend or fiancée.

We care about what is normal to us:

a man and a woman making a life together.

We don't have much room for politics here,

even though we will treat you differently

for all the reasons above and throw in being Black.

Honey, we couldn't give two shits about you.

Can't you see that?

You are a body. A body.

A body. A body.

We are a machine.

Let us fix you.

Let us destroy you.

We will name you dead.

We will reference you in a way
you cannot recognize but must
grow accustomed to.
Some battles are worth fighting.
This is one you will give up on.
It's either you want care
or to be called Walela.
It's either you want care
or to be referred to with
the "correct pronouns."
You can't have it all.
But I'm sure living
would be a nice start.

nonbinary as in

i am not in between
the extreme scales
of being a woman
or being a man
but nonbinary as in
i'm still seen as girl
nonbinary as in
Black is always
a gender first
nonbinary as in
there is a unique
sowing of identity
that's done to
Black people
and I done messed up
all the embroidery
with this new
lil word of mine
—nonbinary as in
chosen name ignored
and dead name
holding hierarchy
nonbinary as in
name changes
ain't nothing new
when Black families

have disowned
the names of those
who enslaved us
this self-actualization
ain't nothin new
nonbinary as in
I am *not* the archetype:
the thin white person
with a short haircut,
wearing short-sleeved,
patterned button-ups
—nonbinary as in
no matter how skinny i am,
i will always
have tits and ass
and who knew
that's all
of what supposedly
makes a woman:
the reproducer,
must marry a man:
the laborer,
must produce more labor,
children with said man.
nonbinary as in
rejecting the roles
capitalism made for us
nonbinary as in
I do not hold
allegiance

to my captor
nonbinary as in
I am still trying
to find the word
that is me yet
there is no word
that *is* me
English,
a colonial language,
a stern muscle
keeping
my words
in check

Disordered Eating Overstays Its Welcome

I can't love my body today.
It's a broken thing.
A compass spinning to nowhere.
I don't love myself enough to believe it.
I don't believe Ivie
when she calls me beautiful.
I do, however, take it as testimony
when someone spits in my face,
"You're too fat to have cancer,"
as if I didn't just throw up my dinner.
Hunched and heaving over a dirty toilet.
"Too fat" sears onto my stomach
when I blow out both my knees working
out and emotional eating turns into bingeing
and it's all got to be invoiced and compensated for.

Believe me, I am trying to not go back there.
To eleven years old, giving my lunch away
to the other kids & everyone calling the
weight loss a blossoming in time for middle school.
Trust, I'm not trying to go back to high school
and counting calories. Five hundred in a day:
Trader Joe's frozen meals,
a half piece of See's chocolate
and everyone calling my body perfect.
Or twenty-two years old and the leukemia

liquifying my fat down and it was a
"Holy hell, you've got a fast metabolism."

Sickness is beautiful until it's identified.
Someone on Instagram said
I was *as big as a house*, therefore
I cannot have cancer.
I taste my destroyed self-esteem
and chew on my tongue for the
entirety of a four-day water cleanse.
Now when I remember that message,
it's done in my own voice.
Or I believe it to be my own thought:
I'm fat. I'm fat and disabled.
I'm fat and disabled
and trans and queer
and Black.
And no part of me
is considered "enough"
and all parts of me
are revolting.

Let's play a game:
What happens to the
fat cancer patient
when they hate their body
so much that they now wish
to be undiagnosed again,
to be in a hospital bed and
their almost emaciated body

is covered in white sheets.
At least they are pretty.
I'm pretty, though,
so damn pretty.
The most beautiful skeleton
the doctors have ever seen.

iMessage Cranks My Eating Disorder to 1000

Grandma dies
Mom disappears
Invasion of the body snatchers
Mother accidentally leaves her
phone at home freshman year
I unlock it in our lavender-tiled
half bathroom, pining for words
of reassurance as if I am indeed
the child she takes pride in:

iMessage:
I hate her
I hate her I hate her
She's such a fat bitch
I hate her
I hate her
She's such a fat bitch
I hate her
I hate her
She's such a fat bitch
I hate her
I hate her
She's such a fat bitch

I hate her
I hate her
She's such a fat bitch
I **hate** her
I **hate** her
She's such **a fat bitch**

scene: a patient attempts to prevent the inevitable

SETTING: Patient sits in their newly assigned oncologist's office down the street from Rodeo Drive in Beverly Hills.

The appointments are overcrowded, patients stacked in a sardine can. The patient is reading the "do you know about your cancer?" posters, holding a notepad, and turns to a door opening.

[ENTER STAGE LEFT] The late oncologist bursts into the room. Slouches and spins on his rolling chair and takes less than 120 seconds to read over the patient's chart.

The patient is keeping count silently, but closed mouths
    don't get fed, so—
doc, I think I got something wrong with me,
see—*lose weight,* he says
I think I got a cardiac—*lose weight,* he says
It's not just about the weight—*lose weight, don't you know*
    how to starve yourself, he says
I think, no, I am sure, this is—*God, when are you going to get it!?*
Your body is your problem, he says
the side effect you warned me about—*[insert dead name]*
    lose weight, he says
that comes with the chemo pills—*if you lose the weight,*
    then we'll see about it, he says

it's a problem now, so what happens if—*listen, listen,*
   you are covered in blubber, he says

                        you are a beached whale who drank the ocean
Okay, doc, but, like, my face, hands, and feet are cactuses
   holding on to water.
When a, I don't know, killer whale is beached, it takes a team
   to roll it back
into the ocean. It relies on anyone nearby giving a slight shit.
   No one blames
the whale, the apex predator, for its miscalculation in
   hunting a seal.
Everyone sees a struggle to survive and administer the aid, so—

Lose the weight, he says. [Six months pass, the same
   medication is prescribed.]

The inevitable hospitalization takes place.

SETTING: East Los Angeles

Chart reads: Patient [insert dead name] has: 200,000
   white blood cell count,
an infection, signs of significant swelling indicate potential
   cardiovascular ailment.

The EKG technician reads a Richter scale, dismayed:
You should've had this done before, like, as soon as
   you got here.

A doctor huffs and puffs, all smoke and no flare:

Why didn't you come in sooner?

The patient sits in a hospital bed, IV in their thumb, hair tied

into a ponytail,

their nails digging into their palm to supplement the desire to curse:

I tried to stop it,

the chemo coughed up my organs onto a beach, and

everyone just kept passing me by.

Authorizations on Medi-Cal Be Like

So you got a health problem, huuuuhhhh?
Well, go to your primary care doctor.
But he's not available for three months.
So, wait, but if it's as big of a problem
as you claim it is, you can always use
the ER as your primary care doctor too.

You speak up.
"I think something is up with my heart."
It's not the first time you're saying this
—but oh, sweetheart,
you gotta go to your oncologist,
we don't do all that here
as your primary care doctor.
But before the appointment,
we need you to go get your own
blood drawn at Quest Diagnostics.
Even with an appointment,
the Downtown LA office has a wait
time of four hours in a dirtied room,
the Beverly Hills office is sanitary and
got less of a wait time—if you're willing
to pay the toll: an Uber. Or beg the people
who claim to be family. Like: your lover's mother.
Your untimely health problems do not fit into

her schedule, but she will do the drive,
your lover will ride along with you,
but they both will be too burdened
by your cancer to come inside too.

Don't forget your oncologist's office
must send the blood-draw order to Quest,
so go early, beat the rush hour, good.
You're in a pristine office,
but the order hasn't been submitted.
Call your oncologist's office,
talk to the nurses. They will sound bored.
They may even dismiss you with exasperation:
"We already sent that."
Only to discover:
to the wrong Quest.
So, hang on,
they'll give you a call later.
Later means two hours.
Later means they done forgotten about you.
Call again.
Your oncologist's nurses will speak
in the tone of a tea-kettle soprano
like they 'bout to let some steam off on you.

Don't forget to be nice.
Quiet mouths don't get fed,
but knowing your rights
will get you dead.

Mama taught you that one.
Know your illness better
than any patient your nurses
and doctors encounter.
Be careful, though,
it makes you unlikeable.
Makes you uppity.
Like you are aware
you deserve better treatment
than what they are giving.

Oh look, the blood-draw order is finally here,
that is: if they can find a vein.
Every phlebotomist will stick you twice
and shrug with a *"come again tomorrow."*
Like South Central is around the corner.
Like your lover's mother takes your health seriously.
Like your lover can accept leukemia is the new normal.
The reality is all of this is a gamble.
When they are able to coax the blood into a test tube
on an undefined future date, then and only then,
you'll be able to see your oncologist.
Take another Uber: $30 just to say
*"Hey, I think there's something
wrong with the chemo I'm on."*
It will be like you won the Olympics of Insurance
when that leaps onto the oncologist's lap.
But no dear, you are just getting started.
Sit down and hear the doc play hot potato with you.
Throw your hands up and let out a *tsk.*

Slap your thighs and say, *"Well, forget it then."*
A year will pass. You done decided to ignore
all the problems. Cuz they ain't problems.
It's a YOU problem. Not a medical problem.
But the emergency room visits say otherwise.
Once again, the ER
a more attentive doctor than your own.

When the Oral Chemo Fails, Part One: TASIGNA

When they tell you the first oral chemo, TASIGNA,
is failing, you will be made to believe it is your fault.
Like cancer is some sentencing you didn't stand a trial
for and the jury knows something about yourself you don't.
The judge drones on: *Why are you this way?*
Punish your body. Starve it.
Smoke down a cigarette.
Hide the smell with the spritz of air freshener.
Everyone kinder than you has died.
Diagnosis is caution tape
and survivor's guilt dissolves it.
Pathetic. Your lover has spent years
waiting for you "to get better."
Your leukemia is holding hostage
all her aspirations, a mudslide of wasted youth.
Either you need to get better—get back to normal
—or get gone to the underworld you belong to.
You've been here before. Trumpet horns
and Ella Fitzgerald's "Summertime"
but the living ain't easy.
There is no normal after cancer.
There is no normal after a chemo fails.
"It could be worse" binds any self-pity you possess.
You inhale curses associated with your name, then
drink the shot down like that's real medicine,
like your attitude is the only reason why your cancer is still alive.

You gotta feel me when I write:
I'm not gung ho about living or dying.
The headlines about Black death remain
Amerikkka's entertainment. What is there to stay for?
The "miracle" of living is simply not enough, for me,
in this hellhole.

Unsolicited Advice

Have you tried yoga?
Have you tried being vegan?
Have you considered going to Mexico
and getting treatment there?
Chemo is a poison, why do that
when cancer is also the poison?
Sounds like you toxic.
Sounds like you should stop taking them pills.
You should try the grape-seed diet
or the olive oil cleanse
or the grapefruit diet
or [list of supplements]
or being "alkaline."
Have you gone before a congregation
and said you are healed in the Lord's home?
Have you claimed your blessing?
Because when you do, then you will be cured.
Have you prayed to every God
in every pantheon under the sun yet?
You really should, but *sounds* like
you want to die since you ain't vegan.
Sounds like you believe in Western
medicine more than what your body can do.
Your body will protect you without any help
—you just have to let it. *Sounds* like you ungrateful
about the way I barreled into you with my ego,

my thoughts, my savior complex,
my need to "fix" a stranger.
Do I have any qualifications?
Absolutely not.
Just a big heart and compassion,
so compassionate that I launch
myself like a rocket of anger
when some ungrateful—
I mean—disabled
person doesn't listen to me.
Me—that's the word.
My advice isn't for you,
it's the Good Samaritan deed
I tell my friends about at brunch,
where we sit in our overpriced dresses
drinking mimosas cuz that is our only personality.
My advice isn't for you, it's to infantilize you,
make you think you haven't tried your best,
make you believe if you die,
it's because you didn't try hard enough
or smart enough. Because I was here
with all the answers. The cure.
That good shit your doctors don't have.
Never mind I don't know your diagnosis fully,
or your medication, or your medical history.
What I do, I do deeper.
I am the attuned and divine.
The One with spirituality
to suck the cancer out of your marrow.
My pineal gland is so decalcified

and you can have your body back as yours,
I guarantee it. For a small price.
How does $2,000 sound to you?

What's that rattling? Me?
No snake-oil salesman
Just someone who is *concerned*,
I'm just, I'm just always *so concerned*
that I can't seem to believe the most honest
way to bear witness to someone is to Velcro
my lips together and when time,
only when it's time, ask:
"How   can   I   support   you   right   now?"
"In   this   moment,   what   do   you   need?"

I Think I Want to Be a Grief Worker

a bee died on a shell i was holding.
my elder took her elongated fingers,
stroked its back, and it was lazarus.

i got a unique relationship with grief,
and that insect and i got more
in common than i'd like.

when i was kayaking in third grade,
a san diego bee stung me.
a softball-sized welt
spread across
the inside of my left arm.
with a pink, jagged seashell,
an adult fished out the stinger
—its host, dead, in the water.

now i'm older
and all the bees are dying.
there are fires turning the sky
tangerine in california.
the flowers are weeds,
but the bees find their way
to the ocean. away from home.
from their hive. from their queen.

there's not much to be said
about self-determination
other than
if given the chance,
we would all die for it,
fleeing a monarchy.

"I want to write rage but all that comes is sadness. We have been sad long enough to make this earth either weep or grow fertile. I am an anachronism, a sport, like the bee that was never meant to fly. Science said so. I am not supposed to exist. I carry death around in my body like a condemnation. But I do live. The bee flies. There must be some way to integrate death into living, neither ignoring it nor giving in to it."

—*Audre Lorde,* **The Cancer Journals**

Please Remember, We Met Before and We Will Meet Again

We met before as a lavender field, left unbothered,
until we drooped and dehydrated ourselves into nothing.
Maybe we passed each other on a plane forty years ago
& our eyes were the only hello spoken between us.
Perhaps I was the breeze, you were a swing,
and we sat together from time to time.
At my worst, I say romance is nothing but
ideas used to rationalize life and worth to ourselves.
With that said, though, I am convinced your name was
supposed to be said beside mine. No explanation needed.
We met before as skipping stones, racing across a lake
then falling to the bottom. It was so fast, but even back
    then we meant something.
I think you were a kaleidoscope of glitter after
    I was a thunderstorm
& we missed each other a few times in that way—by
    milliseconds or minutes.
Maybe we were two stars in the same magnificent sky
& people made sense of us by naming us a
    splendid constellation.
In a different life, you were the hand on my back
    saying excuse me
at a party & I didn't go looking for you despite knowing
    I should have.
Or maybe I did, we kissed, and that was all, but still

we thought of one another for a long time after.
Ah, we met before as messages in a bottle
sailing the Atlantic together.
I don't think the person meant to receive us ever got us.
But we spent hours hugged as two pieces of parchment,
and that has to count for something, right?
Shit, maybe we were once a daisy,
me as petals, and you, the stem,
or you as petals and me as the stem.
She loves me? She loves me not?
Time never bowed favorably in our direction, did it?
If I'm not here, I promise I will return.
Look for Me in the Whirlwind

Bless the Blood

A poison turned wine.

Over a year with cancer
and sometimes I think
I am the elixir of luck,
the highly favored
that my god speaks of.

On the worst days,
I remember I am still breathing.
Call on my ancestors at the altar
with a series of gifts laid out
from when I was discharged:
Dried carnations,
an abalone shell.
Candles. A raven's feather.
A hawk's eye stone CJ gave to me.
I think of my grandaddy.
The one my relatives say I am
just as brooding as, with biting
sarcasm and wit that can still
be charming enough to turn on
a jukebox of comfortability in any room.

I think of my grandmama.
A daughter of East Texas.
She, the sweetest woman I have ever known
but still never took no sass.
On my best days, I try to be like her.
There are so many more names I call on at the altar.
Filled with spirits who sacrificed their bodies.
And this body is in a war with itself. But damn,
don't I know I wouldn't have survived if the ones
before me didn't try to either. My people,
we know nothing of olive branches and peace treaties.
I am lined in hellfire with the inheritance to take back
    what is mine.

So bless the blood. The holy communion.
The most divine, for there is more
than my own blood running inside me.
The bearer of good fruit from the poplar tree.
"God don't give us
nothing we can't handle," my elders remind.
This cancer isn't tempered alone,
so I hold my lover's hands
and pray a little harder.
I write these poems
to remind y'all I was here.
And this thing
was trying to take all of me.
Sweetness,

I am the child of Flowers.
Blooming with a body
holding me
and a soul carrying me.
I am both ghostly and living.
The youngest and oldest ancestor.

Bless the blood.
Bless these droopy,
fatigued eyes
and stiff muscles.
Bless the sapphire bruises
and night sweats shivering.
Bless the IV track marks
and these shrunken veins.
Bless this big ole restless heart.
Bless the dreams my body can
no longer afford the rent for.
Bless this in-between brief bliss.
Bless the love I am trying
to make room for.
Bless the cancer.
God. Bless
the Leukemia
I am still trying
to understand.

"Grandma's Hands" — Bill Withers

"N-now, now, don't go jumping into that pool, you gon' wait on the instructor," she says repeatedly to my tiny self. I say, *"Yeah, yeah, Grandma,"* over and over but jump into the water as soon as she turns her back. She shakes her head and laughs because she has yet another story for my mother about me simply not listening and choosing my autonomy instead.

After swim school, we'd go to a tiny donut shop next door and get sprinkled donuts. Sometimes she'd sit on the ground with me as I played with blocks in a white T-shirt, ruffled sleeves, denim overalls cut off over the knee, frilly white socks, and tiny black-and-white Converse. My grandma, always needing her wig and straw hat before leaving the house, was consistently put together but never too fancy to where she couldn't play with me. That is the kind of sweet intention ingrained in her essence.

Swim school turned into visits at her home, then the nursing home. Ask elementary school me who I'd rather hang out with on the weekend: friends or Grandma? Oh, say less, it's Grandma for me. Stop by Campos Tacos on the way, get her favorite burrito, and a cheese enchilada for myself with rice and refried beans. We'd watch *Judge Mathis*, *Maury*, *The Flavor of Love*, and *The Proud Family*. Grandma enjoyed it for the simple reason that she related to Suga Mama. She, sitting up in her armchair while I lie across her bed. She'd always have king-size Hershey chocolate bars we'd eat together. In those moments, we were a portrait of contentment. She'd let me run around, visit the birds that were kept on the grounds of her assisted living home. I would always run ahead, then back to her as she would strut along with her red walker. She was the best friend I always asked for.

There is nothing like the bond of a grandparent to a grandchild. She is who I also call Second Mama. She told my mama that souls in a family can recycle and felt this was especially true when I would wake up from a nap, climb out my crib, look around, and say suspiciously:

"What's goin' on in here?" as my mother and grandmother drank coffee and ate pastries. I felt like something else was going on because I was left out of it. My grandmother nicknamed me Gertrude Ederle for my desire to always be awake, doing something, usually working. For instance, I would constantly ramble about wanting to be an "afternoon worker" because I wanted to be like the big kids who didn't nap. Always wanted to be ahead of where I was.

From the time I was little, Grandma was my first caregiver. Time passed quickly, as it always does, and the roles reversed. Helping Grandma wasn't a chore; it was the best way I could give love back then in middle school. She'd call me at 3:30 or 4:00 p.m. on the dot each school day with "news"—such as: *"You know those new manicure-pedicure chairs, they're saying in the news they're blowing people's feet up."* I would roll my eyes playfully, smirking, questioning if she was losing it or pranking me. The latter is the correct answer apparently. And so there is the origin of my childlike goofiness. She, my first real friend. Our sleepovers were what pushed me through weeks of school with kids I felt didn't entirely understand me. In many ways, she was one of my first best friends. Even from the time I was learning to walk, I showed it off once, then saved it until my grandma came to the house. To this day, I adore her with all this delicate tenacity she has allowed her daughters and her grandchild to inherit. I want to glide as gently as she did: grace but with immense power as she'd utter, *"Thy will be done"* or *"Life will teach you a whole lot."* Surrendering to learning from the universe but also teaching the lessons at the same time. That was my grandma. Always making sure she had a pair of pantyhose on—that was one thing she *did not* play around about. Said jeans were the worst thing to ever happen. Miss Mary had standards, and yet she maintained assertiveness with humility. On my best days, I hope I've inherited that too.

I still cannot listen to "Somewhere Over the Rainbow" performed by IZ without crying and smiling. I remember her resting day, as she ascended to ancestor-hood. I stood at a pulpit, in a spot many couldn't. Made a somber room lighten up by speaking on all the good she selflessly gave to me and others. Her funeral was the first time I spoke publicly. Thirteen years later, hindsight is 20/20 and it's obvious why I became a writer. We can't talk like we used to, but we make new ways of ringing each other's phones. I kneel before her and pray. There are two photos I bow my head to: One where she's younger, wearing pearls, and has a slight smile on her face—an image of elegance. That photo sits next to a photo of her smiling next to her sister, Jennie—both of them in their Sunday best, hats and all. A blue-and-white fine china milk maiden sculpture on her altar from Solvang; she had given me one, so it was only fitting to reciprocate. Sometimes I look through my phone and find the photo of her, my mother, and I because it's three generations at once and I wish that youth could teach us reverence sooner than death can teach us the same lesson. To this day, I hear her everywhere, in the way other Black grandmas talk as I pass them in public. Once, I saw her "doppelganger" at CVS. A Black elder hunched over her cart in a dark brown jogging suit talking in hushed tones with a matching friend in the: pantyhose section. I like to imagine that's her way of saying hello. I gingerly greet both women and keep walking, knowing my first best friend is still here.

The Black *Parent Trap* but with Grandchildren

"My granny V's birthday is the day after mine.
She wanted my mom to hold me in, but—"
Stevie starts.

"Wait, so that means she's born on April 17th?"
I ask in disbelief.

Stevie lets out a *"mhhhmm."*

"That's the exact same day as my grandma Mary!??"

Black people rarely meet in moments of joy
—Stevie and I are not exempt from that.
Los Angeles Police Department don't
recognize another murder as murder.
A Black woman allegedly committed suicide
"willingly" on *their* clock—the footage
conveniently missing. The officer, therefore,
will not be investigated. Los Angeles's billionaires
Caruso and Soboroff smile smugly while gliding
out of a room erupting into misery and disbelief.
This was where I met Ivie too. That is being Black, huh?
To be in a room full of unknown names gulping for justice.
Crying and shaking. And I am trying not to do the same.
Holding in, as I hold out the palms of my hands.
Ask a stranger to place their hands in mine.

Ask for their name: Stevie.
Ask for us to Breathe In
—Breathe Out—
Breathe In
—Breathe Out.

It's gon' be okay.
You know how to get
home from here?

Now we are here years later,
able to turn to each other like
the two versions of Lindsay Lohan
revealing long-lost twinhood.
Our eyes widen, and a massive
"Oh my God" is what's leftover.

What are the odds?

True—Stevie and I aren't related,
but coincidences don't exist with our people.
We get signs, from the water, or the ground,
or the hawk circling up above,
or our elders talking through us
—sitting on a brick stoop outside—
one, Granny V, still here.
The other, Grandma Mary,
standing behind me
with her translucent silver cane
hanging over my shoulder.

"Fast Car" —Tracy Chapman

In the chapel of an Airbnb,
the Almighty Jesus Christ
is watching from a framed
portrait in Lake Arrowhead.
Stevie and I drink
a jug of blood
from the Son of God.
Air guitar and mimic
the guttural pain in
Tracy Chapman's voice
singing "Fast Car."
We ask the Holy Spirit
to keep on driving us
to a blessing we ain't seen
but give us the strength
to believe it is indeed coming.
Prayers don't always
gotta be started with:
Our Father
who art in Heaven,
hallowed be Thy name.
Prayer can be a Black lesbian
singing about taking care
of everybody but herself
and wanting to drive,
without a map,

to the middle of nowhere.
The destination,
any place without
her second-guessing,
and the karaoke
choir sings along,
shaking a vigorous
yes.

Eight-Year-Old Me Has a Dream Come True: Stevie, Ivie, and I Find a Puppy to Adopt

I watched *Snow Dogs* twenty times. The closest I ever got to snow was at the Culver Ice Arena or through encyclopedias I'd read at school. My mom only liked small Shih Tzus. I was tasked with walking them, and I believed if I tied a dog to my Razor scooter, then somehow I was Cuba Gooding Jr. mushing in *Snow Dogs*. Bless the soul of creative children who have absolutely no forethought, and bless the adults who stop us from our own mistakes. But I wished each birthday over numbered wax candles for a *big* dog. Adulthood, to me, was an ultimate aspiration because it meant that if I had a big dog to walk around the neighborhood, then "I made it."

Nova is advertised on a pet adoption website. A halo of light shrouds her tiny black head with tan eyebrows—a German shepherd–Doberman mix. I don't need any more information other than *where do I go to sign the paperwork?* And *what's her name gonna be?* Oh yeah, *Riley*. We like Riley.

Ivie and I drive out to Hawthorne and pick her up, ready to fit her into a red nylon collar the size of my wrist. I carry my puppy in the extra fabric of my oversized sweatshirt. She pees on me and I don't care. I hold her with more caution than I have ever had, lowering her eight-pound body into the bathroom sink. The warm water runs over. Wrap her in a beach towel and hold her to my chest. My mother did the same for me in the hospital, and all this is making me realize: I could never handle having a child. If this is a shred of what maternal love is—overwhelming adoration, devotion, and unending protection. That kind of love can be destructive or healing. The kind that can change the trajectory of a whole life.

Ivie and I Open the Memory Box, Part Two

yellow, green, blue, and pink Post-it notes we paste around
    the home for each other
—you always wrote of loving me more than nature
    could find fathomable.
I keep all the ones you wrote in our desk drawer cabinet.

raffle tickets from the fundraiser we had at that house
    in View Park.
a friend took a video without us knowing, you leaned forward,
kissed my forehead, then gently curled stray hairs behind my ear
—an 8-second loop I hope plays forever.

an apology note confessional admitting you have neglected me
and thanking me for the boundless patience since the
punching-a-wall incident of 2017. the note's signed with a
"you deserve so much better" in red ink that's since
darkened to a worn maroon-brown.

Shai's "If I Ever Fall in Love" vinyl,

the black journal with red pages and an ACAB sticker on the front.
inside: our plans for community organizing and debates on theory
and us sitting hip to hip on the sofa with *The Boondocks*
    playing in the back

a mini Stitch doll from *Lilo & Stitch* because we both
    related to him.
feeling without family except with each other.

2 tickets to the Prophets of Rage show
where we got to meet Tom Morello backstage,
watched Vic Mensa perform "16 Shots,"
sweated onstage in matching black bomber jackets,
screamed with adrenaline outside when the show was over.
dancing remains our youth attempting to process all this loss
and nothingness. thankfully, we still got something here.

Death Interrupts the Shred of Normalcy I'm Finding and Announces: Everyone Black with Cancer Keeps Dying

Black Panther was played by a Black man fighting cancer & the world gasps when he, who was meant to be invincible, dies. The world does not want to acknowledge cancer as a disability. The world calls it an insult to his memory. Disabled is considered a slur. As if the truth is too inconvenient: A superhero can be ill. A superhero can die. A superhero can be more than a superhero: but a person, a Black disabled person.

Chadwick Boseman is not T'Challa, he is Chadwick. But Twitter won't let that go. Twitter wants to prop up his casket as the embodiment of strength. Twitter wants to twist meaning into a competition related to productivity—"If he could do this through advanced-stage colon cancer, what are you doing?" Twitter wants to use him as a means to tell people like him. Me. How meaningless we are if we aren't making meaning out of our cancer. If we aren't superheroes. If we don't suffer in silence too. Like admitting the disease as truth out loud makes us weak.

So Chadwick Boseman's death becomes less of a memoriam to who he was and more of an ode to productivity. An ode to how much we can give on empty. And a disabled person's death becomes a talking point to delegitimize other people like him. Because a king could never have cancer. A successful person could never have cancer. How dare we say such a thing.

Tell me, what does that communicate to the kids who look like me?

Be quiet. Work yourself into the ground. We don't care about your symptoms. We don't care to feel sorry for you. Stop feeling sorry for yourself by admitting the cancer is alive. Why can't you be more like him? Like Black Panther? Like T'Ch-Chadwick?

We promise there's a beautiful grave waiting for you. We will give you the best internet funeral when you are gone. You will inspire the masses for your secret, but before you die, we will make fun of your appearance. And we will speak on your behalf. Then, and only then, we will mention cancer. We will utter the word *cancer* to tell others, just like you, to silently bundle the diagnosis in their cheek. To chew on the diagnosis even if it's like glass claws tearing through your flesh. We will give the eulogy: *If he could do it, why can't you?* A myth. All because reality is too hard to believe: He couldn't.

He couldn't do it. He had cancer. And he died. He died. He is dead. Your king. A beacon of your Black excellence. Has died of cancer. Your child will learn their first Black superhero is more mortal than we like to be comfortable with. And *that* is why we are gathered here today.

Crip vs. *Crip*

Rest in Paradise, Mac

Crip (noun): Slang for a disabled person/the whole of
    the disabled community/
a school of thought
Example: "I'm on crip time"
Meaning: Time bends differently when the universe that is
    my body dictates it

Crip **(noun):** A Black gang that originated in Los Angeles
The word can be used in reference to a gang member or
    the gang itself
Example: "Nipsey Hussle's death made gangs, including
    Crips, unite in grief"
Meaning: Black is still Black no matter if you wearing red or blue

I heard the word ***crip*** for the first time
when I was kid cuz I got family from South Central.
And there are gangs and manufactured wars
and crimes of survival. And there are ***crips***
who are **crips** and don't know it
—like Maccapone, a man who was protective
of the ways death finds organizers. Was known
to wrestle with the pigs at 2 a.m. if it meant another
one of us got home safely. He, steady waving
a large Pan-Afrikan flag while carrying

175

a "No Justice, Fuck Peace" sign
right out in front of the Crenshaw Mall.

He offered himself as a shield to me
with "You good?" when I was 23
and tryna get home without being harassed.
Offered a "You good?" when I was 24
and working my first short-lived job
after my diagnosis. "You good?"
was our "I got you."

When Mac dies after having neurosurgery
in another South Central hospital.
Another hospital that churns out death
more often than remedies even after the discharge.
When Mac dies, my grieving—all our grieving—
is organizing and activism. We, all so young
and naive back then but committed to liberation
or self-determination or to call something ours,
to name the oppression that hung over our heads
with acidic rain. We wanted what Mac wanted:
something better.

In 2019, I saw the word **crip**
used by someone who didn't bang on Twitter
—wondered if the hood was being appropriated yet again
& questioned if they don't understand how in South Central,
you don't wear blue cuz you ***crip***.
Red means blood, and as the numbers
on the street signs get bigger,

the colors matter more.
So don't wear nothin' suspicious
unless you want a: Where you from?
Meaning: Who are your people?
Meaning: What street you live on?
Meaning: Who do you know that we know too?
Meaning: You better answer and quick
before—

In a parallel reality,
crip is an invitation to community.
I am told it is a positive reclamation of disability,
at least I think so, or so it seems some weeks,
and other months I am exiled for simply being a "negro."
Meaning: I am too audacious for saying being Black
and disabled is real different from being white and disabled.
Meaning: Solidarity sometimes ain't functional.
Meaning: There's a quick snap to delegitimize us
Meaning: We go quietly into a purgatory

So what would it mean
to be a Black **crip** in South Central Los Angeles,
for a disabled Black child in 2019 who isn't a ***crip***
and yet somehow both will be synonymous
with: danger.
Meaning: You ain't safe no place
Meaning: You ain't welcome nowhere
Meaning: Where are you *really* from?
Meaning: Who do you actually belong to?
Meaning: Who are you without a name?

There is a duality of language.

I don't claim crip cuz of how I learned it.
My family, music, Mac and the Rolling 60s,
the Jungles and BPS, my fiancée and her twin
wanting that "hood aesthetic" so bad,
my best friend actually living on the street
where drive-bys happen so often
—there's a permanent vigil,
and this shit prolly don't make sense
to a lotta y'all, right? It's not meant to.
There goes that duality of language again,
the double entendre,
the one foot in and another out.
I'm just over here trying to jimmy open
the door to my imagination.
Meaning: Where do I go to find
the name for where Black
disabled people
belong?

Survivor's Guilt

For Tonya and Alana

It is lonely to be the one who still survives.
Guilt makes a shameful sorrow of me.
There is no amount of music or screaming
that can reverse a prognosis—
why do I place my Hope in the survival
of other Black people? Selfish of me to cry
when I should backflip that I'm still alive.
Waking up should be enough,
but other people have tried
harder than me to live.
Darts carrying suicidality whiz by.
How do I unbury a tomb and trade places?
It hurts to stay. I imagine it hurts to die too.
My tears tired of crying.
How am I supposed to practice gratefulness
while swallowed in this deep hurt?
I am exhausted with the burden
of outliving the sick people I know.
Dear God, you fight dirty.
You drink a forty ounce and trip over your cruelty.
Kill the wrong people and allow for corruption.
There are widows with beds that still have
the imprint of their lovers, parents burying children,
elders no longer sitting on the stoop.
Dear God, how are we to believe in love

when you aspire to murder it?
Were we a case study gone wrong?
Dear God, I better hear you say illness
is an accident and you are working
on resurrection being offered
to more than just your one
prodigal son.

Social Media Is a Bitter Wasteland

Synchronize your mandible to us.
Don't sound too Black, too angry, too urgent.
Do that code switchin' you were taught instead.
Sympathy is the sad clown makeup, so get up.
Post an autobiography as a flier tryna get by.
A cartoon with you and all the trauma that
can be exploited for a dollar listed in bullet points.
Message any person who got a following larger than you
and ask them to share your life with even more people
to scrutinize and aid you. This is your job at the end of the day.
Since you [your immune system] couldn't keep one.
Material needs don't get paid for without hustle.
Some people care, genuinely, and see support as ongoing
because cancer is ongoing. These are the kind of people,
my friends, who slide you extra money when dappin' you
up in person or order you free boxes of Blue Apron and
bring you a pack of herbal salves. Work alongside you
to help reach more people, whether they got a blue check or not.
Whether they got 200,000 or 200 followers. Others with access
will ignore you, leave your message on read. Others with access
will make you a charity case. Rely on you for their public image:
*"That's such a good person, sharing that flyer and following
that poor cancer patient's Instagram."* You don't got a boss
to report to, but there are bills. You don't got a boss, but there
are people who donate and demand access to you
   under any circumstance.

Others who donate do it without strings attached. Will not

    ask the invasive:

Did you get money for groceries? For deliveries on the nights

    you cannot cook?

For the Ubers to the doctor? For the car note? Money

    stacked for emergencies?

If you go to the ER again? Get hospitalized again? If cancer gets

    even more unpredictable,

are you prepared? You got enough bank to cover

    Ivie's mom's emergencies?

Did you get money for those new clothes since your pants are

    bursting at the seams?

Where's the money for Ivie's musical whims? The guns that she

    won't stop talking about

and the militancy she has to have and cancer has robbed us

    of enough, right?

Virtual reality dictates the present one, so watch

    your tongue anywhere.

All your business is ours. Everywhere. So do not get offended

when your condition becomes a figment of

    the public's imagination.

For Whitney Houston

Kevin Costner stood behind a pulpit in his Sunday best at Whitney Houston's childhood church, mourning her death. He shared the story behind *The Bodyguard* and how he knew instantly he wanted her involved even though he was asked, *"Do you realize she's Black?"* He noticed early on that despite all the talent she had, despite all the beauty, she was still insecure. Still asked, *"Am I good enough?"* To which many would click their teeth, thinking, "How could one of the best singers in the world be insecure?" And sure, that's easy to think about as I bit my lip watching. But I, personally, was trying not to cry as he ended his speech with: If he could tell Whitney something today, it would be, *"You weren't just good, you were great."*

The day my body decided to act like a plunging roller coaster, I was dizzy, trying to "sleep it off." Whitney sang me to sleep. "My Love Is Your Love." Fred Hammond's "No Weapon" woke me up. With every hospitalization that followed, Whitney and Fred have been played.

Whitney was our play-pretend auntie—especially after *Cinderella* with Brandy. Her voice could go from a saintly falsetto to belting, sustaining breath longer than I ever could. She had this dynamic personality and a vocal range like her singing was the gateway to heaven itself. Yet she was told by family, by lovers, by too many surrounding her and benefiting off her: She was not good enough. In fact, she was crazy. Then the public agreed. To have hardship and be Black when you are supposed to be "just a singer" means to lead a life pretending no one has tainted it. Was ridiculed for having a toxic, then abusive relationship. Only because it distracted from the singing. I know I've said it before, but to be Black is to be nonhuman no matter how much money our talent makes us. It's to supersede expectations to only be told, *"Do it again but better."* Her addiction made her bad stock, loving a woman made her a heathen, the abuse she endured made her a nobody, and support was never considered something a "strong Black woman" needed. Everything was always Whitney's fault—never those around her. She took the hit each time.

I am no Whitney—nor will I ever be, but I do cry about her often lately. It seems no matter what we do as Black folk, that is the question that lingers: *"Was I good enough?" "Why wasn't I good enough?"* After listening to Kevin Costner's speech, I sobbed to her Grammy performance of "One Moment in Time"—snotty nose and all. Because you can hear it. That eagerness to be something meaningful.

I think we all can relate to Whitney. I collected the gigantic tears from my face in a bottle of wishes, thinking, "That is all I want, too." One moment and I can die in peace. Just one moment where everything is falling into place and I know I am gonna be here. Or see for certain that I have left an impact. Or a part of my heart has lived on in another. That is all I notice. I tend to ravenously search for through cancer. Before cancer. Probably after cancer.

If anyone could speak to me as a self-loathing child, if anyone could speak to me as a self-blaming adult, I would want them to say while I am alive to hear it, *"You aren't just good, Walela, you're great."* I want to do the same in return. I don't want to be thirteen years old, picking rose petals off the bouquet sitting atop my grandmother's coffin at her funeral, thinking of everything I wish I could have told her. I want to receive flowers while living. I want to give flowers while I am still able. I don't want to rely on being good enough by someone else's impossible standard. I want to be good by my own standard, in my own time. I want to be great, I want to be good, and I want to fail.

Perhaps if I'm wishing real hard, I want to be half of the sunbeam Whitney was. I want to evoke the type of emotion with the sound of my voice that makes you jump into the human form of yourself and say, *"Gah damn, ain't it wild to be alive? Ain't it wild to have all these emotions and actually feel them!?"* I want to know about love. Like how bell hooks writes about it. I know love is far more vast than what a romantic partner can give me. I want to love people, and I want people to experience my love. I want to understand love in all its forms; I want to stop begging for love, for the bare minimum; I want to stop being afraid of giving love. I want to give to others a fraction of what her music and films, like *The Bodyguard*, *Waiting to Exhale*, and *The Preacher's Wife*, gave to me.

No, Whitney, you weren't just great—you were brilliant. You are brilliant. And any good thing I do is for the kid singing along to "My Love Is Your Love" on a silver portable CD player in the back of my mom's car, looking out the window for love to find us both.

"Bills, Bills, Bills" — Destiny's Child

So much of cancer is trying to find the meaning of life.
Those pursuits are for people who can afford to travel
and check off bucket lists and have doctors who care
if they have low morale. The meaning of my life,
at the moment, is reduced to green sheets of money
cut into $5s, $10s, and $20s. But I'll take the spare change too.
I'm a vending machine for pity. Throw me a silver dollar
and watch how I have to exploit my own sadness.
That is what keeps a roof over our heads:
people dropping change or checks as I virtually
hitchhike the internet. Bruh, I'm not tryna be ungrateful.
I wouldn't be alive without the kindness of strangers.
It's just when everyone knows you because of cancer
—that's all they want to know you for.
My "sad"-ass, sick life is an autobiographical poster.
Being Appreciative and Ashamed are the two lanes
I straddle with ember-clouded eyes while logging
in to social media. I never wanted to do any of this.

    "Have to
    will make you do
    a whole lot of things
    you don't want to."

Cancer and the Illusion of Choice:

My friends don't really ask me if I want to go out anymore because they know the answer is going to be no. My oral chemotherapy does not make me the "fun," "spontaneous" friend anymore. I am cautious. Being in a long-term battle against cancer is consistent change that is not on your own terms. The amount of people willing to pause their lives was different in my first couple months with cancer compared to now. Now I am approaching almost two years in the fight—most people have compassion fatigue and are over it, and I understand why.

Cancer is a daunting experience for everyone involved. If I had the option to simply move on from it, I would try to as well. Cancer has put my life on pause, and I am empathetic to those around me who want the option to move forward: whether that means going out without me or planning for and working toward a future that they know is more guaranteed than my own. And of course, who am I to make everyone around me experience the same isolation and stagnancy as myself? That's a recipe for other people's unhappiness and resentment, and I don't believe in demanding my loved ones to be as unfulfilled as I am. So of course, when my partner wants to go to a rave at eleven p.m., I'm going to say yes, because who am I to deny what seems like a cool-ass experience AND I'm going to be asleep anyway, so who cares? Each time, I smile and encourage all my loved ones to do what their hearts desire, what makes them happy, and usually that's rooted in a sense of belonging around other people—and of course, I genuinely want that for them. But when the phone call ends, or they leave my house, or when I go on social media and see moments of joy I wish I could insert myself in—I cannot help but feel jealous. And so I lie in bed and say terrible things about my body, this illness, and I am embarrassed by the lonely.

I am often angered by my inability to have options. To have autonomy. I so desperately want saying no to going out to be MY decision because I simply want to stay inside, not because I HAVE to due to my health. I'm constantly compromising and bartering with my illness in ways even those closest to me do not understand. And I largely don't talk about it, for I don't want to make them feel guilty for realizing my version of balance is wildly different from theirs; my balance is rooted in largely giving up what I love for the sake of surviving: my career traveling as a poet, organizing at the same capacity as I used to, going out, kissing whoever I want, running errands at Target without a panic attack, etc. Even recently, with getting a Vogmask meant to help filter the air of bacteria and toxins, I guess I was convinced I was superhuman and able-bodied, took things too far, and got sick again. And so I'm writing this from my bed with sheer disappointment in how even with what's meant to support me, there are limitations.

To be honest, most of my resentment comes from understanding this form of balance I'm forced to adhere to isn't necessarily living. It's just existing in hopes my cancer might have an expiration date sooner than later, if ever. Now I'm almost two years on chemo, my cancer is responding relatively well, the progress is slow and dips up and down, but I am still being forced to continue on with a choice I didn't make. I've considered having a stem cell transplant but now am too scared given that I watched a fellow young disabled patient, Claire Wineland, die shortly after her lung transplant. She was young, white, thin, had visibility—it should've worked for her, and it didn't. I cannot imagine how it'd go down for me.

The past year, I've deeply considered stopping treatment completely. I want to live, travel, go out, organize, do whatever the hell I want, and spending the rest of my twenties on a hope that by thirty I'll be cancer-free is really not enough most days. Most days, the idea or the opportunity to make choices, be independent, be autonomous even for just two to three years, and then I'm gone is a fantasy that outweighs everything else. I'm not afraid of dying—I'm afraid of dying battling this illness rather than living with it. I'm terrified of spending however many years making choices for everyone's comfort but my own, everyone's happiness but my own. I want chemo to be *my* decision, and that's something I'm working on with a therapist. What does it mean to take something back from an illness that takes everything away from you and the repercussions not be too big? What does it mean to find a community while being alone most of the time? What does it mean to live on your own terms when your cancer makes the rules? What does it look like to be independent when your illness makes you dependent? How do I find happiness in the midst of all this? Once I am able to answer those questions, I'll know what I want to do for myself confidently and proudly. And the decision will be my own. The choice will be my own. And I won't be doing it for anyone or anything but myself and my future.

The New Oral Chemo: BOSULIF

The full moon
has unconscious
rationale.

Once a month,
spanning seven days,
for four weeks,
my nerve endings
circuit-break
and a blood vessel
pops from tonight's
dinner g'ttin'
upchucked
into the toilet.

Nightly,
my stomach is a traitor.
Forgets to lock the door.
Insomnia breaks in after.
Disassociation sweeps
my consciousness
up in the air at three a.m.
A bird's-eye view
from a jellyfish
pillowed cloud.
Pain as Ritual.

The Bad Black Stressed-Out Cancer Patient Who Leapt Through Time, Part Two

(inspired by *The Girl Who Leapt Through Time*)

I haven't wanted a cigarette in so long,
but after my support group,
I ask a friend to pick up a carton for me:
Marlboro Red 100's.
I just wanna smoke one down
and feel the regret later.

In 2016, a former friend's father, a therapist,
compared smoking to deep breathing.
It is self-soothing in the worst way.
Years later, I pace a sidewalk by
the Slauson Swap Meet holding
all of what can kill me and inhale
—I got contempt for whoever thought
it was a good idea to let me exist.

Imma probably smoke the whole carton
cuz I can't predict anything I will do
when it comes to this type of self-harm.
Yeah, go on and judge:
I am not a compliant patient
in a medical system that is not
compliant to preserving life,
so really I'm just helping

them do their job, which is:
rationing my care
[or]
speeding up the inevitable:

Don't worry, babes,
we all die anyway.

I'm Noticing Chaos and Sex
Are What Ivie Thrives On

I stay up and watch her sleep on a sand
pull-out couch in the living room.
Her lips slightly parted, with a couple locs
covering her face as she snores.

I rest my head on my palm and leave much unsaid.
I been scratching what I wanna say into a journal, though.
The theme for the last six months:
"I stay pulling Ivie out the trenches of herself."
"There's a double standard between the promises
I keep versus the ones Ivie doesn't."
"She punched a wall again." "I don't know if I can do this."

I fear we are two compasses with our norths opposite of the other.
I was her Polaris at one point. I was a love worth
      adventuring toward.
We went out of town the other week. Got an A-frame cabin
      in Lake Arrowhead.
Hoping a mountain and nonpolluted, noncity air would clear us
      of our problems.
But those were still waiting back home, and she still had gotten
      what she wanted:
eating pizza at a restaurant like that time in DC in that hideaway
Airbnb where we ordered Domino's, danced to
      Tinashe's "Party Favors,"

and were equally enchanting to the other. We were hilariously
　　reckless back then.
But we were younger then, and I thought we were growing
　　older together now.

I am pained by the ways in which our different feelings toward
　　desire have left us.
Lover, you speak of all this untapped potential, and I am
　　convinced you are brilliant too.
Yet there is always another lie. Followed by the monotonous
　　I'm sorry.
Followed by handwritten letters that were once romantic.
I want you so much, but when we hold each other,
　　there's infinite distance
—not our own galaxy like back in 2016.

You are my first and only real beloved, so if that means handing
　　myself over to you
because it is the closest I can get to you . . . that you let me get
　　to you, I will do so.
I've served my body on a platter to other lovers before you.
　　This is not any different.

Ivie's Family Had to Pack Up and Move to a New Spot and Now We Live by the Marathon Store

We got put in a shed with near nothing working, and I don't know if that's an upgrade from an attic, but I still pay the rent. Ivie's family got possessions of their own. Meaning I see some of the family members' eyes glaze over. Snatch money out my pocket and resent me for giving or resent me for reasons Ivie only knows. This family can be an architect of drama and diversions.

We got a barely working shed behind a brilliant home and I don't see it as a screw-over. But you gon' be willing to overlook a whole lot when it's the first time a roof that feels like your own covers your family's head. A place for our family: one puppy and two wives.

I make excuses for all of Ivie's family, but appearances often are as simple as the dirty house on Degnan, the dirty house on this new street. There is no place that is not filled with copious amounts of dirt.

Ivie told me she saw a demon once when her family lived in Lenny Kravitz's childhood mansion. A woman died in the front house sunroom on Brynhurst where Ivie's brother slumbers.

There is no place that this family has chosen that has not been haunted.

We live in a backyard shed turned tiny home. An afterthought. A silhouette of a woman breathes against the window of Ivie's mother's bedroom. A fog descends on the property. This family and their vacuuming of souls that do and do not belong to them, alive or dead. The spirits follow and inhabit our dreams as waking insomnia.

When We Left the Old House on Degnan

I found a pile of almonds in a glass bowl.
"It's an offering," Ivie's mother said.
None of the animals touched it.
"It's an offering," she said.

When we all began moving out months after that,
a worker from the moving company asked
if a man lived with us. Insisted on seeing
a silhouette in the second-story window
and knocking at the door.

I do not doubt him. I knew the man.
He was not my kin. He was an angry
drunk with a seething stare after eleven p.m.
His domain was the first floor.
The only bathroom available
for me to use was the one downstairs.
Come nightfall, I'd rush,
skip steps, full bladder, from the attic.
Skid across the kitchen in my thin black socks
to lock myself in the bathroom. Hold my breath,
wash my hands, then sprint to the attic.
I was afraid he could walk through me and possess me.

He wasn't the only ghost in the home.
There was a lady in the attic. She would
observe me when I'd sit at my makeshift
altar in the morning quietly
burning herbs—I think she was hoping
someone who knew her would light
a candle and call her name
so she could go to her real home.
Not here.

I often wonder why beings haunt places.
There were always other ghosts who came and went.
I would cleanse the house for hours with what elders taught
me and a shekere Stevie's friend from Brazil gifted me.
But those two: the man and the woman.
They always stayed.
Both with unblinking eyes.
But only one terrified me.
The man with pupils bulging,
searching for ways to get his hands
into the material realm,
readying himself to take a bottle
of wine over somebody's head
on the wrong or right night.

Déjà Vu

I know winter in Los Angeles
has come when my mental health
swan-dives off a forty-story building.

Well, actually,
I've been depressed since November.
Somehow a new year made it worse.
Happy 2019, I guess.

I play *The Sims 4* in a house with no heat,
and I can see my breath, a type of fog,
in my visceral daydreams:
Noose around neck and me
hanging in the archway to our kitchen.
Feet dangling, almost too serene, and
it's captivating. Or sometimes,
there's a white claw-foot bathtub
and what is supposed to be water
is blood I bathe in.

I don't think I can trust myself.
I plead with Ivie to stay with me,
like the many nights I stayed with her
—when I'd hide all the sharp things
and watch her sleep. But
it all time-warped me back

to April 9, 2017
—begging her to come home.
Texting through my dizziness,
"I think something is really wrong."

I am not offended when she does not stay.
I'm too far gone to consider
maybe she despises me.
A violent intrusion into her livelihood.
It's tiresome living in the shadow
of someone trying to live so loudly.
I watch her walk to work at that
coffee shop down the street instead.
The girl will be there,
the one she's been lying about,
brown-haired, wavy, thin,
with feline hazel eyes
and the aroma of possibility,
lust, and sex. Whiteness
is a crown Ivie bows to.
She rises from kneeling,
and it makes her callous.
Makes me want to crawl
out of my skin. Rip off each layer,
lose sixty pounds, grow out my hair
—be as seducing as the tempest
who can peel my love from crisis
just in time to steam her latte.

The Aftermath

Ivie deems my suspicions paranoia.
But I keep dreaming about her lying to me.
How can Faith blossom when the seed is a rotten lie?
I need to trust her, I know,
goddamn, how come every time
I try to write about myself, it's about her?

She left me. Alone. All the sharp things there.
A processional already crashed through the living room.
I call the suicide hotline. The cancer hotlines.
I email this one therapist who worked at my cancer support
center.

Place my weight—pounds stacking like bricks,
drop them atop my hands—therefore all the things
that draw blood cannot be touched. For once,
I am frantic about trying to live, and no one notices.

Except for Riley,
a four-month-old puppy,
guarding me from my worst self.
I hear the quick pitter-patter
of her paws. She places a tug toy
into my lap, her head on my knee.

As if to say,
*"Please
don't leave me here
alone."*

The Crisis Hotline Volunteer Calls the Suicide Hotline

Have you ever seen yourself hanging between a doorway? You're dead and you don't panic because it's serene. You almost go looking for the rope because you want to stop feeling this crazy and look like the version of yourself in the doorway. So you start pulling on your hair. You want to scratch your eyes out. But instead, you punch your hand into a wall, and it's swollen green and blue with memory. You sketch UGLY into your left thigh as a reminder that this is what cancer has reduced you to. Your medication makes you swell, and so you convince yourself it's because you're fat. You convince yourself if the cancer didn't arrive, then everything would have gone differently. That this kind of suffering wouldn't know your name. But still, every time you open your eyes, there you are. Dead. Swinging in a doorway. And you want to go up to this mirage of yourself. Touch them. And maybe it can become a portal. You just want to see everyone you've lost again and stay there. That would be paradise. Your heart starts pounding in your ears so loud. You text your partner to come home from work. But she is avoiding you. So you are alone. In a small house. With your thoughts. And dead you is still in the corner, and it seems so much better than anything cancer can give you. Anything this life can give you. You pace back and forth. Your mother's voice disguised as your own encourages you. Reminds you how you haven't amounted to anything: *"What makes you think now, at twenty-four, you will be anything remarkable?"* You tell her [yourself] she is right. Fifteen-year-old you appears out of thin air, their arms covered from self-harming, and they are gaunt from the disordered eating, their eyes vacant like the day you got diagnosed, except fifteen-year-old you laughs. Says, *"Funny, we worked at a crisis hotline, and we can't handle ourselves during a crisis. What should I play on our phone when we die?"* Your breath becomes panicked, and you run to your phone sitting on the bed. *"What is the suicide hotline number?"* 1-800-273-8255 blazes across the screen. The phone rings, a man answers, there's a beat of clarity, dead you is gone from the corner, and you blurt out, *"I think I want to kill myself, but I have therapy for the first time next week. I think I should try that, but waiting is becoming hard."* Fifteen-year-old you nods and leaves out the front door. You collapse onto an orange chair at the foot of your bed. Your hand cradling your forehead. One foot in this world and the other foot slipping into a pile of nooses— everything snapping shut with a crack.

I Send God a Voice Note

Tinnitus in my ear rings to the haze
of cicadas in a Louisiana swamp.

The whole of my spine becomes electric needles.
Up for seven days, a magnet for pain.
Do you mean to tell me that all this frantic
effort for living was traded for gasoline?
My last memory, a shredded white flag.
It's the last photo of my optimism.

Don't forgive me, Father.
I was born into a family of sinners,
in a world full of sinners,
was meant to be nothin' but a sinner.
Ain't none of us pure, including you.
Including me.

God,
I have been both the saved and the damned
—I can say I hate both.
Have you seen it down here?
A cannibalism of morality
raging inside
of Capitalism's Junkyard.
Black people get shot by the pigs
and it's business as usual.

A mass shooting happens and
the vigil is yesterday's news.
I am afraid of all the speculative fiction
stories becoming accurate premonitions.
Everyone is glued to their cell phones, watching
nature enact revenge. I know you've seen it.
Heard the prayers too. The ones whimpering,
"It didn't have to be like this."

Dear God, is that a ringing in your ear, too?
Like all this suffering is losing its meaning to you?
Man, it's my first prayer in a minute, but for once,
can you let us wake up to a kinder world than this?

This Is My First Therapy Session in a Minute, Part One

I came here because I think I am crazy.
Well. That's obvious.
I think my lover is not satisfied with me.
She lies, mistruths slurring from her mouth.
I wanted to die, I think. I didn't threaten it,
I just needed help. It's too much on her shoulders.
My partner, Ivie, is so messed up from my illness.
The sink is full of maggots. Sometimes,
I wholeheartedly believe she sees me as the cancer.
An extension of control and greed.
Oprah had an article about how, like,
50 percent of couples break up because
of cancer, and we used to say
pishposh, that won't be us. I don't want it to be us.
So I guess that's why I'm here now.
Sitting in an office off North La Brea across from you,
a cross-legged white man with a long brown beard,
six feet apart and—*Damn, his gaze sees right through me.*
I don't know, I don't write poems or songs about her anymore,
about anything really at all. I think whatever resilience
I've got left is postmarked to the wrong address.

This Is My First Therapy Session in a Minute, Part Two

I'm bloody honest and someone is concerned about me for once.
For once. I'm not batshit insane. I mean, then again,

    I'm out my mind.

I just don't think everything is as much of a mirage as I'm told it is.
My new therapist apologizes on behalf of those who failed me.
I wish I could live in this office. Linger as I order my Uber,
in awe of four walls and plants filling it like a small jungle

    of seafoam pots.

Forget the sound of music, the sound of nature is the

    small fountain raining

a meditation when I allow my ears to guide me. Allow

    my therapist to ground me.

I find myself in a creek without shoes. My therapist

    smiles, close-lipped,

observing me. *"For the amount of trauma you've experienced,
you are a deeply self-aware person."*
I don't have the word for it. But I think this is . . . safe?

I Have Highs and Lows in the Thirty-Minute Uber Drive Home from Therapy and Ignore My Ancestors Again

YouTube recommends a Sofar Sounds session;
an electric guitar begins picking on a loop
designed to strike my optic nerve.
My eyes make misty-fogged glasses.
YEBBA allows me into her mind;
by the end, I encircle myself in a seance
of used tissues. Snotty and ugly-crying,
YEBBA writes what I cannot.
A wail that's so rageful while harmonizing
with unanswered questions.
Can you tell me what I've done wrong?
I feel like I woke up and the rules of our
relationship changed.
I'm tryna understand you,
but I don't want to when I keep catchin' you in
the lie hidden on your phone.
You told me to go to therapy.
Is revisiting my childhood supposed to distract
me from what you do when I'm not around?
Do you still want to be engaged? "Fake-married"?
Let me know but don't hold me up;
I don't want to hold you up either.
We both made promises, remember?
I've lost your priorities.

You wanna be poly and I agree

after rereading *All About Love*,

but I still dream of you cheating on me.

My great-grandma Can sits with me in the Uber:

"Baby, what is dependency on a love committed to deception?"

I've got no good reasons left. I've got every good reason left.

I am dependent on you in a way that I don't know how to explain

because who goes through shit like this as young as we are?

You seep into my spinal fluid, and your approval

    is my sustenance.

I can't answer Great-Grandma Can because I feel like

    I'm betraying you.

I paint a bolt across my mouth, and I have never been so rude.

My teeth, charms on a bracelet you made for me.

A talisman or a hex depending on the day.

I cried at the dentist today.

Exposed my bottom row of crooked bones to the kind
    lady's masked gaze.
Like her daughter, I am the faint memory of war.
Her accent divulges she knows of men like my
    East German father.
Men with beer-belly stomachs hovered over saucepots
& Wolf Biermann's guitar strumming to "Ermutigung."
Men who taught us how to break jars open with knives
    & cooking as vigilance.
We slam metal to the pop of a fastened jar and hollow-gasp
    for trapped air.
Last night, I screamed for similar ease.
Instead, I was given dreams of my teeth falling out.
My back molar fillings disintegrated inside a
    Glendale dental office.
I wheezed at the mercy of a loving stare.
My dentist recognized I have my father's mouth & finite enamel.
My face spent January practicing new ways it can wear despair
like he and my oma once did. Her ex-lover's fists pummeling
their skin through drunken fits. My family tree is made
from the corrupted veins inside a runaway bruise.
Love doesn't have to put its hands on you to destroy you.
We are bursting bloodred tomatoes and violent parades
    of chipped teeth.
Empty, numb, and mindlessly cooking to avoid our idle sorrow.

Running On E

Running on empty.
Running on the search for rejuvenation.
Concrete pavement got me
running to dance circles,
heavy with the aroma
of conjure oils and shea butter.
Blink to the percussion of drums,
and I forget about the cancer.

So I'm running on hope.
A man grabs my hand outside
the neighborhood coffee shop and declares
I am no longer sick. I wish I could be that foolish.
So I'm running on trying to forget.

Running onto the Metro rail.
Riding to the beach with Ivie
—we sprawl out on a pink towel, play mancala,
and fall asleep under the sun.
Do a fast walk to Bigg Chill and get that
vegan cookie dough on the side—saying,
"Yeah, them white vegans got this right."
Snap a photo and we are blissfully enough.

Until drywall collapses under
the weight of yet another mistruth,

and the world will only pause for me.

Running on denial.
Running on the rupture and mundane
—and it's bleak.
Papier-mâché rooms,
Medi-Cal check-ins where you got
five animals gnawing,
eating you from the inside out,
and the doctors want you to pick one
cuz *"we don't got time for all that."*

So now I am running on compromise.
Running on self-sacrifice.
The other four animals make a den inside my liver,
chase my palpitating heart.

Running on back-to-back phone calls
to my insurance, my doctor, my insurance,
then to authorization offices, back to my doctor
—a merry-go-round in reverse,
where everyone's time but my own matters.

So I'm running on the Metro rail again.
Except this time to a cancer center
filled with white women older than myself,
their entire lives resting in their crow's feet.
They baby me for being so young:
"You haven't been able to do anything."
No shit, I know.

This used to be helpful,
but sometimes . . .
One of them tells me to be more grateful,
her words lined with the kind of good money
and good insurance I don't have.
I sarcastically express gratitude,
then disappear for months.

Running on anger
and how inconvenient it is to everyone.
I am thin air and repressed grief.
I work myself like a massive construction drill
with no thought of the damage.
Like the biopsy, I got pain everywhere,
so just let me get anywhere but here
before I suffo—

Running on circles formed outside
after open mic nights in Leimert Park.
Sharing a bottle of Henny
or a joint
or our odd sense of humor
—walking back to the house I stay in,
and when my friends come over, it feels like home,
but they leave.

So I'm running on empty.
Running on lonely.
Running on sleep & its allure.
I wake up looking forward

to being unconscious again.
Guilt-ridden hands rest before my altar
—I can hear my ancestors: *"Tsk tsk tsk."*

Running on disconnect.
Cutting the umbilical cord to myself
and all those before me.
They were taking up too much space in my head.
I don't hear them, and it scares me sometimes.
Nothing seems better than complete solitude,
so I consequently do the unthinkable
& banish those whose lives were given for me.

Running on ache.
Ache is eager to pluck the violin strings
of my mind. I don't scream as I begin
splitting myself in half. Turning myself
into a crossroads, chasing life and death
at the same damn time
—I am truly the worst thing
that has ever happened to
everyone around me.

Running on Blame
and not knowing where to set it down.
I carry Blame as if she were my first child.
Tend to her so she knows to cry for me
before anyone else. I sing a lullaby:
*"Call me when you want a home to rest in.
I am but an empty cave. Make a bird's nest of me."*

Ambivalence toward Sex

If I am not enthusiastic
about crawling across
the floor,
bowing at Ivie's legs
to make our bodies
sandpaper,

then that means:
I do not love her.

I do love Ivie.

I do not love sex.

I do not hate sex
    . . . it's just a thing.

I hear Society spit
out its Erewhon juice.
Society will start soapboxing
about sex, questioning
if chemo is ruining my libido.
In middle school,

I wasn't interested in having sex.
Wealthy white boys yelled
about it being what seals the deal for marriage.
Each regurgitated whatever their siblings,
parents, TV, porn, the internet
told them:
body as
a cavern for sex,
agency as
a chamber,
and if love
is to be considered,
one must follow the steps.
Cosmo taught us "girls"
never to question.
I mean, what gives us
the "right" to be this "difficult"?

I do not understand this side of myself.
I try to cast it out by "making love."
Yet I'm grown now and Stevie
mentions asexuality,
but I don't think that is an option
if I am to stay engaged.
That day in middle school
course-corrected me.

Am I to be doomed
like what Moses Sumney sings of?
Seen as a hiccup in the human experiment?
The crackling static
of a broken television?
An error
until
fixed.

Beast of No Wild

Home of no name.
I was born into a world
naked and shivering.
A heartbeat given to me
by a tornado. Alone with
family alive. A still earthquake.
A burning train headed to nowhere.
Born to be a contradiction.
I am all this sorry flesh asking to be loved
and never believing when it's here.
Everyone has been a liar once,
including those whom I love most.
I don't trust myself. I curse the sky
for dissolving the moon. Make gods
of things that die. I am the most
solemn violet drooping in a rainstorm.
I can turn life into poison. Watch me
feed myself pills meant to both kill and save.
I am the most self-aware sadness.
There is no antidote.
I zone out instead of zooming
my fists through a wall.
The lesser of two evils.
Daughter of tornado hands.
My face is my mother's,
and I try to mosaic myself unharmed.

Beat my eyes into a desert.

My organs weep, and I don't ever cry no more.

Ain't no place safe for the scared Sacred child in me,

not even these poems. I ain't wrote in a minute.

What is there to make beautiful

in the ordinary that is Suffering?

My therapist asks me to describe my self-blame

Where is it located?
What does it look like?

Smooth blue stones
lodged in my sternum
and behind my eyes.

"Can I speak to it?
Or can you speak
on its behalf?"

I agree hesitantly.

"How long have you been here for?"

"Since Walela was eight years old."

"Were you invited?"

"No."

"What is your purpose?"

"To protect Walela from pain."

He asks for the name of the stone in my sternum.
I say: Clarke.

"Clarke, what will it take
to dislodge you from Walela?"
and I couldn't really answer.
All the saliva in my mouth
turns gummy
—he inquires
if we could draw me
in relation to the stone.

I take the crayons and draw
a full-body portrait of myself.

"Do you have anything to say to the stones?"

"No . . . well, thank you for protecting me,
but I need to let you go to move on."

My therapist begins to describe
the type of protection the stones
gave me. In a world where an
eight-year-old could not fathom
being so hurt by those around me,
blaming myself became necessary
for me to survive.

"Where is the limit for this kind of self-abuse?"
"When do you stop torturing yourself?"
"Are you ready to move on?"
"What would it look like to not
have the stones anymore?"

"Relief,
then an overwhelming sadness,
then rage because
I will have arrows drawn
with pinpoints for exact
landing."

April 9, 2017: Twenty-Four Hours Before the Cancer Is Named

A clock with no hands,
yet Time does not hold still.
You were out
when I called,
carrying a nervous need:
*"Come home,
I think I need the doctor."*
You didn't come despite
the promise that you would
before you walked out the door.

Later, you explained,
*"I thought it wasn't that serious.
My ex used to do that."*
You never saw what happened
when we hung up:
the house spun ten times faster
and Whitney's gospel
warped inside my ears.
Your mother patted
my back in the dining room,
insinuating I was doing the most.

I inhaled baby carrots and haggardly
held on to a peach soda
like it was the last call at a bar,
waiting for you to come home.

But my emergency could wait.
From then on, everything could.
My life was your worthy gamble,
and who wants to admit you are
a roll of dice to what you once
believed was a steady love?

The Heart Interrogates Me and My Trauma

What does the bottom of an ocean feel like?
Was the sinking slow?
Did your reflection follow?
Do you praise it?
Why do you not believe yourself to be holy?
When did the cancer become you?
How does it feel to be Judas?
Why does cancer give you a kinder beating
than the one you give yourself?
Where do questions go if no one answers?
Where does God exist if you stop praying?
How old were you when you first hated yourself?
Did cancer make you remember?
Does your body not feel like your body?
Where is your home if not with yourself?
What made you forget the word *mercy*? *Holy*?
What does the bottom of an ocean feel like?
Did you forget how to breathe?
Does cancer hold your breath for you?
Is the ocean a metaphor?
Do you just want to be invisible?
Do you just want to forget?
Is the surface the hospital?
Is the surface the dizziness,

the biopsy, the catheter,

the racist doctors, the advanced directive,

everyone crying at your bedside and

you having to pretend you aren't afraid of dying?

Are you afraid of dying?

Is a tunnel of white noise easier than me asking?

How do you forget the things that demand to be remembered?

When does a trigger stop being a trigger?

When did cancer become you?

When did you start believing cancer is

the worst part of learning how to grow?

How come your eyes are a desert?

Why would you rather beat your heart numb?

Who hurt you?

Who forgot you?

Who made you feel this worthless?

How did you get here?

Where do questions go if no one answers?

Messages in a Bottle Lost on an Island Shore Somewhere

July 7, 2018:

Text Message: To Mom:

I did not even ask to be born to begin with.
You disowned me before I disowned you.
I know you don't care, but I am making
the leaving mutual so I am not abandoned again.
I'll pretend we are not made from the same covenant
if you do too.

February 22, 2019:

Text Message: To Mom:

I know it's been a while since we've talked.
I wanted to say thank you for bringing me here.
I'm doing better; I don't know if it matters,
but I'm in therapy now and it's been working.
You don't have to respond if you don't want to.
I just guess I miss you. Love you. Always.
Thank you for teaching me everything you did;
it got me to where I am now. I'm sorry
I didn't see the sacrifice sooner.

May 12, 2019:

Text Message: To Mom:

Happy Mother's Day. I haven't heard from you.
I'm not good at taking hints, but I think your

silence is meant to say something.
If I meditate for long enough, Grandma
and Papa cry about us. Maybe
we'll find each other again in an abyss.
Next time in Zion, not Babylon.

Psalm 91: Papa

You know when Dave Jr. enters the room even as a spirit. All my friends who are spiritual practitioners agree he be the loudest in their ear. *"Loud and bougie. He real bougie."* Personality-wise, at times I am his mini me. Or so I've been told. Boisterous. Grown into the scorpion he was. He is the air of dignity that follows me when I enter a room. Dave Jr. was not one to be disrespected—that's the type of shit that would make him cut you with a wineglass with such ease, leaving you stunned and a soaked maroon. When I first talked about my grandpapa to my lover, he pushed her shoulder as if to say, *"Don't mess with my kin."*

A crest of brilliant metal and swords, he will protect even in the afterlife. And he will do so with panache, wearing a tilted ole school hat paired with a Coogi sweater. Oh, and don't forget the gold. The watch. The cut of his cheek that has been passed down to me. I nod to him in the morning, his photograph: a selfie taken with a Polaroid camera. With dice, cash, coins, and Hoyt's Cologne beside his photo. He remains a man of effortless cool, an embodiment of a golden generation in Black Los Angeles. Looking at his photos reminds me to do more than take care of myself—but to indulge at times. To get myself all put together to go absolutely nowhere. Kick up my heels knowing I deserve to do things without explanation. As long as it makes me smile.

Smile like how I would when I was younger and ran up to his apartment's door. Banging on it without regard for anyone around me just like a little human would. He'd deepen his voice and say in a gruff boom, *"Who's that knockin' on my door?"* And it would get me every single time. My smile would spread to occupy my entire face. As I let out a squeal of laughter. That's the type of joy he wants for me.

The days I adorn myself with his gold medallion, I make sure I am wearing a fit worthy of his approval. Just like how he once carried a photo of little me in his hat, I carry a medallion with his initials engraved. Apparently, anyone would know I'm his grandkid from how we'd both attempt to unionize our coworkers. Acting on labor injustice. Without question. And that's how we lead, many times impulsively. It makes us feel like we are stuck at the bottom of a well. Sometimes from that bores brilliance, and other times it simmers into frustration and lots of unkept jobs.

He and I were not able to spend as much time as I wished on this earth together. But for the short amount of time we were both here, it was a blast. In the morning and evening, I bow to a glass of water on my altar. His, with a deep mahogany cross sitting above it. I remember the day his Bible arrived at my apartment. His presence was palpable as I exhumed it from the packaging. Psalm 91. A hawk lands in front of our home on his birthday. Always my watchful eye.

Who My Mother Reflects

Grandaddy
before he was my grandaddy
was not a good daddy—
wolf of South Central,
then Cheviot Hills,
then wherever he could be.
But it wasn't Wall Street.
He took money that
didn't belong to him.
Promised a private school
education to Mama.
She'd shift through
letters of acceptance,
her golden ticket:
Congratulations,
you're not going.
Yes, he was a sweet man,
but he was also a man,
and in Black families,
brutality is passed
down in more ways
than one.
Mama promised herself
she'd never turn into him.
Grandaddy saw the grandbaby,
me, as a do-over. A do-better.

Mama spun me up into
a wheel of dreams for herself.
Entangled me with the web
of her aspirations and demands.
I am but her dream deferred.*

*"Harlem" by Langston Hughes

Chosen Love Heals and Breaks and Heals and Breaks My Mama

Great-grandmama Texanna is not my blood great-grandmama. My great-grandaddy Dave Sr. remarried, and it was to a fly woman who wore fur coats and cat-eye glasses, with hair down to her waist. She could roller-skate with my mom and aunt and hold on to her leather purse at the same time. Never to be seen outside without lipstick on: Texanna was that girl. My great-grandaddy was a patient man who I never met. My mother would speak fondly of him and his marriage. How when she was a toddler, my mom would sit in my great-grandaddy's lap and insist on splitting raisins—her slobbering toddler mouth biting a small, dried fruit in half and pushing the rest into Dave Sr.'s mouth. Each time, he would never spit it out but emphasize how good it tasted. My mother and aunt would take trains out to San Diego, and as their grandparents got older, they became the caregivers, especially my mother.

There is a pattern in my family of the children developing bonds with grandparents, who often see the babies as a second chance. My mom and aunt were theirs. When my great-grandaddy had to get his leg amputated, my mother was a teenager and took any class that would teach her how to care for him. She didn't see it as losing her youth, but returning the love her grandfather gave without any expectation. That is how love should be. The father of her father, he was the man who indulged my mother's toddler antics. While they share the same name, Dave Sr. was always more gentle than Dave Jr. They look back at me from a sepia-toned photo from when they were going to church: he sitting up in a suit and a fedora, and Texanna with her arm in his. Both of them dapper, but Texanna the real star.

Both of them died before I knew them. Tragedy doesn't unfollow Black people because we've done enough time with it. I don't remember how my great-grandaddy died, but Texanna I cannot unremember. Left the gas on before going to church, came back ready to cook Sunday lunch, and the house blew to smithereens. She was flung into the street around Christmas, her favorite holiday. She'd decorate her and Dave Sr.'s home with Christmas trees, Christmas plaid, stockings, Snoopy ornaments, and tinsel. This woman was the real Santa Claus and his elves. She died not long after. I better understand my mother's anger masking her grief around November and December as I lightly tap the Snoopy figurine roller-skating in Christmas red-and-green on my altar.

I imagine my mother felt similar to how I did when my grandparents died: left behind by the only people who understood her. A lot of family photos used to sit boxed in my mother's closet because she was too pained to even look at them. Hope is bleak when loss enters when we are so young. But each Christmas, my mother and aunt would change the home's interior design, the smell of fir trees lasting from December to January. Great-grandmama Texanna and Great-grandaddy Dave Sr. sat in the armchairs on either side of our living room's tree on December 24 each year. We couldn't see them stuff the stockings. We all were asleep while they ate the cookies I would leave out for Santa. But come morning, they still sat in those armchairs, waiting to see all generations of their grandchildren turn on the Disney Christmas parade, brew coffee, and eat chocolate Danishes from a bakery down the street while the boom box played "Little Drummer Boy."

Three Generations in a Frame

I was inside
my grandma Mary,
for I was inside
my mother
when she
was waiting
to be born.

Three generations
inside my grandmother.

We, her first loves:
first daughter,
first grandchild.

There is not one
picture in my family
that can document this.

We, the first
to frame a photo:
eldest to youngest.

Smiling. Alive.

Not lost. But known.

Daughters of the Dust.*

Daughters of the Dust by Julie Dash

25 Things I've Learned before Turning 25

1. No one is going to advocate for myself better than me—there is nothing wrong with that

2. Boundaries are essential, and it's important to enforce them, including with myself

3. Love is not showing how much of myself I am willing to sacrifice to prove I am worthy—this may have been normal earlier in my life, but I need the people around me to love me for ME

4. Rest is okay, fatigue is normal, and it's not useful to run myself into a ditch

5. Being principled is hard, and there is such a thing as being "too principled"—when it comes to rationalizing WHY I am deserving of being mistreated

6. Self-care, for me, requires discipline. I must understand why it's so hard for me to place myself first.

7. Family does not define my personhood

8. It's okay to remove myself from toxic people, especially those who financially or emotionally leech from me

9. Gaslighting intentionally distorts our reality—truth is still truth and my feelings are still valid no matter if people shy away from or manipulate themselves out of accountability

10. Raising a puppy is HARD and is a lesson in patience

11. I am afraid to ever have children, for I've never witnessed one family that isn't toxic

12. My trauma is my job to heal, and when I do, I am effectively healing generational trauma

13. Therapy is work and work that is worth it

14. Other people cannot dictate what my needs for support look like

15. I am more compassionate than I give myself credit for

16. It's my duty to not let people take advantage of that compassion or exploit it

17. Love is a choice to heal together

18. I am a very good facilitator and an excellent listener. I wish younger me knew someone like older me back then.

19. My rage is when my hurt is too afraid to cry

20. "Tears that don't fall make the organs weep instead"

21. Mourning my childhood is okay

22. Depression and cancer often go together; it's okay to curse the world for surviving

23. Surviving is a constant battle, but I am one brilliant warrior

24. My purpose is forever tied to liberatory work

25. In a world full of sorrow and doctors playing guessing games, I made it to a day many thought I would never see, and thus I am a whole-ass miracle

Magic Survived My Mother's Attempt
to Annihilate My Memory

September 1997:
a kid in oversized denim overalls,
a white shirt, slicked-down black hair,
and a face more concerned with reading
than the two children standing beside me.
We are lined up in front of ferns
with branches snaking up
the white brick wall of our school.
My tiny hands wrestle
open a flimsy red-and-white book.
Nothing in the photo is legible
except for the word:
magic
with an exclamation point.
My grimoire,
a passport to places
film cannot capture.
The place I go when
I write to you
sitting here.
Reading me.

Photographs Carry More Historical Weight
for Black People than We Are Taught

My grandpapa took the original selfie.
Not Paris Hilton.
It was Dave,
cuz he had that Polaroid camera
pointed at himself
and grinned into the film.
He didn't come from money.
Photo shoots?
Those are rich-people luxuries,
and, well, lookee here,
here's luxury
in the hand of a man
born of farm laborers,
and he is the agent
of how he wishes to be perceived.
Both artist and muse—
propped against
the shadow of himself,
he briefly emerges
as a man of little complication.
Dave in red and black,
eyes closed like we got
in the way of a moment
between him and God.
Blessed be for him.

To be Black,
emerging from white film
cooling atop the kitchen counter,
and see himself
created in his own image.

Taking a Picture So We Can Forget the Conditions and Remember the Moment

There's a meme that says,
"I want to smoke with every
perception people have of me."
And I laugh while I suck the
last smoke out of a rolled herbal
blend of lavender and mugwort.
No, I am not happy with visibility.
The magnification of my plight
turned into thousands of people
who know my name, my @,
my story—you know, the one
about the kid with the cancer
and the partner, the adults,
the system that don't really
help 'em, so they fundraise?

I do not bite the hands that feed me.
Images are concocted and demands
are made of what they want from me online:
the requests keep clogging my inbox.
I traded in my agency
and am getting lost in my survival.

Tonight, Stevie yells we deserve more than
what other people want to outline for us.

Yes, we can be Black and _____. We can
exercise the right to celebrate
my twenty-fifth birthday.
The home decorated with purple, black,
and gray balloons like Sam from *Danny Phantom*.
The guest list, a Rolodex of friends from NYU
to Los Angeles to South Central to Koreatown.
In a tiny home behind a bigger home on Brynhurst,
we pack the place and heat sizzles in the middle
of a frigid LA winter. We dance to replace jackets,
we light up and it reflects humidity,
we drink and warmth coats our breastbones.
My inhibition dances on the table like in *Coyote Ugly*
and yells the lyrics to "I Write Sins Not Tragedies."
For once, I am not overthinking
tucking my belly in
to "make me look less fat."
We all know that shit don't do nothing:
I am fat and not covering myself up.
Got a crop top with no bra on
and vertical-striped pants.
Wrap my arm around Stevie's shoulder.
They got on a *Naruto* graphic shirt,
and we both disabled, Black, and neurodivergent,
both rejectors of gender.
Someone asks to take a Polaroid of us:
being ourselves is unprecedented,
and there are consequences to perception,
but we pay that no mind.
We let a camera flash.

Sing "Happy Birthday"
because one of us made it to twenty-five,
and we don't give a damn about the neighbors.
Polaroid film cools atop the speakers
blastin' "Racks in the Middle."

Five Feet Apart (2019 film)

"I get it now, it's really hard
what you're going through."
That's the epiphany that
becomes the theme of the evening:
trying to understand each other.
One as a patient and one as the caregiver.
The Grove has their lights dangling at night.
We walk beneath them, bellies full of vegan
burgers and milkshakes, our arms interlocked.

We watched *Five Feet Apart* hours earlier.
Stella was the closest "me" we could find
in recent years of "chronic-illness cinema,"
a white girl with sandy-blonde hair
and light eyes, with cystic fibrosis.
Equally capable of the same precaution
followed by self-sabotage as me.

I roll myself into Ivie's nook as we cry in the theater.
The most understood I ever feel
is when I can tell a memory is being formed.
Tonight, I look to Ivie's tall frame.
Repeat *"I love you"* while walking down Fairfax.
Ivie's arm is protectively draped over my shoulder.
I look up at her profile,
the forefront to a polluted Los Angeles nightscape.

But the cars don't make any noise.
They are nothing but confetti of light.
The most beautiful thing Ivie
gifts me are moments of empathy
—where I can padlock my heart against
the shape of hers
and we both swallow the keys.

On Generational Trauma:

"Trauma skips generations until it reaches someone able to heal it. And when they do . . . they heal seven generations back and seven generations forward."

—*Unknown*

I am born into a brilliantly sad family.
Depression holds every other generation between its teeth.
How ugly it has made my family to have razor tongues.
Abuse has been the only way they know how to grieve.
If it hurts, they punch it into the daughter.
The daughter punches it into the next one.
So it is no surprise I am born when it is raining
while carrying generations of trauma on my shoulders.
My back mirrors the Middle Passage as blood
from the womb drips off it. This is the first mourning.

My father, a quiet bystander seeping in white noise.
A man who fled East Germany, changed his name,
and knows nothing but bounty on his head and erasing history.
My mother does not think I am her daughter when I am born.
My father, unsure too. Both say I look too much like
a being of my own. My grandmother says that's because
I've been here before. The elders in my family flock around
me in adoration. Attempt to convince my mother to let me
leave with them. My mother, their daughter, with bruised hands,

does not know where to place her sadness. So as I age, she forces
it into my chest, then calls me too sad. My father deserts me with
his body still lingering in middle school. Now my mother's body
is no longer who I claim as my first home. And so if home is not
with him or her, then where is it? I say my elders, I
   say my grandmother,
who I called my real mother. She dies when I am thirteen.
Grief enters my mother's shadow and hollows her empty.
I am my mother's keeper who does a damn good job.
I keep her sadness as a lockbox in my chest
and speak on behalf of my family about how to celebrate life
in the midst of Death. And the gospel chords on a piano
   play softly in the back.
But my mother stops being my mother and terrorizes me
   until I am twenty.
Death has a way of unhinging monsters in ourselves, so
   I don't recognize her no more.
But I still bring myself flowers, meaning I still search for
   my grandma's spirit
as refuge for us both.

My grandma's sister becomes my keeper.
Hands me a gold elephant ring and says
my words are what give me my power.
She waits until I am the last face she sees
before her spirit retires from this world.
My mother convinces me I am a bad thing,
and this is how she copes—by projecting her sadness
onto me. Says it pisses her off how much we look alike
because she wants nothing to do with me.

I want a better life for myself; call poetry my liberation.
My father kicks me out, reminds me I was never really kin
to the white people in my family. I become a being to hold
my parents' lonely. Both been running all their lives.
A daughter reminds them of what a car crash is,
and I am their collateral damage.

I am hurting myself with those who love me like my parents,
meaning not at all. Depression been had its teeth
in my neck since I was twelve, and it has taken
everything in me to not die. Trauma continues hunting me.
Finds me by way of addiction, of poverty, of betrayal,
and all my ancestors scream.

By the time I am twenty-two,
I am a moon full of craters.
But still I call myself beloved.
Find flowers to dry
and say my grandma is still here while
wearing her sister's ring. Pull myself
from the wreckage in time to meet my
love of loves—Ivie.

Never have I known such intentional tenderness.
The first place the crying child inside me
can call home. This is love of biblical proportions.
We both choose to heal as I give her my ring
in a time when my body is failing me.
We haven't even seen a year together when the
doctors say the cancer is killing me. My mother

comes back and loves me like nothing happened.
But still she leaves me every night. Ivie
is the one who sleeps next to me, and so
she is who I call my family. Cancer wants so bad
to hollow me like my mother and father and make a cycle of me.
This year, I wanted to die. Said what is the point of healing
when my own family won't do it too?
If my parents won't celebrate me living?
If I have to pass this all down to my child?

My partner holds my heart and squeezes it.
Says, *"I am your family now"* and
"Your healing is owed to you regardless."
So I put the knife away and ask for a dream
instead of me dying. I am good fruit born from a rotten tree.

I tell my therapist two days before my birthday,
"I don't want to die," and he says, *"It's a brave choice to live."*
My doctors say the same, and I know my grandma agrees.
This year is the first time I have attempted to celebrate myself,
where I have been proud of myself to have survived myself.
I believe this is the first step to making amends with trauma,
to making my ancestors' jobs easier,
to restoring a bloodline back to honest,
back to holy—I am them,
meaning I am Spirit's handiwork:
a miracle indeed.

Megan Thee Stallion, aka Tina Snow,

aka H-Town Hottie is in my computer right now.
Myself and the other Black cancer patients
scream & she cries & there's an undercurrent
of understanding among Black folk about cancer.
It takes and we still give. The computer speakers rattle
with the vibrato of elation from survivors and those
    in battle alike.
I don't remember what I said to her. I know there was a thank-you
for the love she carries for the women in her life,
    her grandmother, her mother.
There was a thank-you for loving us enough to spend time with us,
knowing we isolated. Feelin' like what is the point some days.
But today is not one of those days. Today, every Megan song
is good enough to dance to. Make my booty clap to.
When I'm alone, I unstiffen and dance like I once did
    in middle school.
When my body wasn't something for men to sexualize.
That's why I dance alone now. No thank you, sir, keep it pushin'.
Gyrating my hips ain't an invitation to push up on me.
Ain't nobody can tell me I look busted because boooyyy,
I look geeewwwwddd. In a Palestine shirt. Wearing sweatpants.
And the temperature in my apartment pops like the grease off
Granny's skillet making breakfast and coffee on Sunday mornings
before church. We all say *"Praise be to God"* in different ways.
I praise dance across my living room, dripping in purging.
Oh, Happy Day.

The Nail Salon as Self-Care

Glory be to the nail salon of Black women yelling at *90 Day Fiancé* and *Temptation Island* on the TV. Our nail techs file profusely to carve out our nail beds for our next installation of art. Glory be to communing as strangers in the familial conversation.

Ode to the claws that keep us alive, to our nails sayin' *"I'll cut you"* before we have to utter it. Joy to the child who once got cuticles pushed back and light pinks chosen by the mother to coat the nails, now a quarter of a century old, finally getting what all the grown women in my family got.

Praise nails as a rite of passage. I inherited the ritual here in these salons.

Peering over my mother's nails at five years old with eyes wide to the French manicure. My mother's style mimicked from my grandmother's.

Glory be to the start of each month, the acetone nibbling on the glue connecting myself to whatever went wrong last month. We throw all those nails away. We hail the nail salon, for it is where a world of options extends before us in a way society doesn't provide.

For two hours, not one thing exists outside these four walls. Everything simply does not matter.

My hands are maneuvered gently out of the purple UV light. The drying of who I choose to be for the next month and a half.

Thick almond-shaped French-manicured nails, long, with gold charms of the sun, moon, and palm trees glittering on each finger.

Not exact to the tradition, but it's still a ceremony of sorts. A small means to keep on.

That "For the Love of You"
by The Isley Brothers Type of Love

At a beach in Santa Monica,
you convince me
there is a tiny island
in the distance,
but the island
was in a velvet
box with a small ring.
A stranger walks by us
hugging and says,
"Oh, propose already."
You throw your head back
laughing, holding up my left
hand with an emphatic,
"I just did!"
Los Angeles in 2016 didn't need
any stoplights that night;
we were whipping through
them in green on the Expo back.
Snuck into the Jacuzzi of my Downtown
apartment complex. Played The Isley Brothers'
"For the Love of You" as we kissed
over and over, practicing the slow dance
for our eventual wedding night.
My first serious relationship,
first engagement, first true love.

My world became a universe
of bubbles foaming around our waists
atop a watery chamber of eternal fidelity
and forgiveness.

Driveway as a Crossroads

Stevie does not judge me
when I take out a pack of cigarettes
and light one. I exhale. The nicotine
gives a small head rush.
We both try to avoid Ivie's phone.
I know what's on it. Saw it.
Polyamory as excuse for a type of cheating
she thought she could "explain away"
with rationalizing or a tantrum. Except now
she's catatonic and her mother is holding her.
I whisper to Ivie's mother that professional help
is needed because there's something else goin' on,
more than an all-nighter can fix.

"I mean, she said, 'I've done nothing but
be honest with you during this entire process—'"
It's not dark enough outside to conceal the derision
etched into Stevie's face. I found everything:
the secret texts to that white girl about meeting
at a rave that I spent hours doing Ivie's makeup for.
There are the messages oozing
with compliments and insecurity.
Her pining after a girl she once made fun of.
But Ivie always made fun of the people she loved.
After all, I am her best punch line.

We lie back on the cold concrete,
our eyes plastered to the unknown.
Stevie does not know
this is when they became my best friend.
Sitting cross-legged and exchanging stories,
waiting for morning. There's no rushing
to figure me or Ivie out tonight.
Tonight, Ivie is with her mother.
These few hours we will take and make about us.
Even if it's a distraction. It's for our benefit.
And tonight, we deserve at least that.

The Breakup

I don't give myself enough grace to say what I want. So when I said I wanted you, I thrusted my hope on the chopping block that night. You, a nervous butcher and I thought I stopped giving myself to shaky hands years ago when I met you. Desire is constant, love is practice, and you liked the idea of it. My poetry made you feel like melted glitter, and you proposed to me. Did so every day after on one knee. Until years later, I was shivering on a dock, looking for you as I plunged into ice. You, too scared to follow me down into honesty—despite the times you fantasized in the songs you made me. But songs ain't conversations, so I'm not gonna say you loved me right now.

You asked that I climb your castle walls and live up to every good thing cuz I said Imma do right by you. Shifted myself into whatever you needed me to be. To have us, I had to discredit myself. I made our world as kind as I could with our limited options. Simply because I loved you. Shrugged my shoulders, wrote you into the sky, and it was easy. Loving is easy. But your self-sabotage made all of this hard. The nights I went to sleep knowing you would not be coming to bed because some other girls, girls who are not sick like me, were giving you an ounce of their time. We had everything, and yet I lost all I once knew to be true about you in the confusion you brewed around polyamory. Three years in, you talked about playing it safe in the face of losing me.

But you drove off in that white girl's car, and I took the biggest risk when I finally said,

"You broke our boundaries when it came to that one girl. So. I can't do this. We are going to live apart; I will put you up in an Airbnb and you can have time to be with whoever you want and figure out if you want to be single or married."

An unreliable love is worth the risk of rapture.

The Suicide Attempt Is Kurt Cobain's Heart-Shaped Box

No more slouching toward the moon.
A bottle of honey drizzles the sky.
Sunlight as a chorus of boundaries.
Until the front door is slammed,
then
the closet door.
A gun cocks back,
a chain locks itself around my ankle.
The heaviness indicative
of what is to come,
and it's a *Crash*,
then *Shatter*
of glass
rhinestones.

Stevie,
weak, iron-wristed,
flies a chair through
a double-paned window.
Adrenaline
breaking an entrance open.
The only thought possible
is *"Don't let her finger
press the trigger."*

In high school,
this photo from
Kurt Cobain's suicide
was shared on Tumblr.
I had never seen a gunshot
wound to the head.
He was not identifiable,
a pile of guts seeping in thick fluid.

I beg of you baby:
"Do not disappear
into the tempting void.
Take the gun from out
beneath your chin,
and instead hold on to me."
In the car, you repeat:
"Every day it feels like
I am chewin' glass,
I am corroding
from the inside out."
I'd rather you speak what you feel
than be taken by a bullet of unspoken turmoil,
my love. Your mother whispers Bible verses.
Your brother hides his tears in the rearview mirror.
I, numb at the center of crisis,
a statue of doom:
a storm cloud with gravitational pull
over my head, and it rains obedience.

Clink.

I am fastened to you.
If you fall,
you will take me with you.
I cannot ever leave you again.

My Nervous System and Leukemia Link Up and Take Their Revenge Out on Me

Next day. Tennis-ball-green bruises greet.
Small mossy mountains on my shin.
I will deal with this cancer crap tomorrow.
Today, I'm driving to the beach and dancing salsa later.
Please. Let me have one good day, I plead
while tapping on the lumps as if they are remotely
interested in listening. Dizziness pantomimes as vertigo.
But I am ready to frolic out the front door with Stevie.
I am willing to ignore the alarms my cancer is pulling.
Until
that ringing in my ears,
the one from two years ago,
taps against my sound-bowl eardrums.

Shit.

"Heard It All Before" by Sunshine Anderson Takes My Mind off Going to the ER

Sunshine Anderson is the gap-toothed
shawty giving the soundtrack for a
scorned partner. My mom would flip
her on while driving down Pico. Her singing
a replacement to cussing my dad up and
down the street. It takes doing a lot of wrong
things to be able to relate to Miss Anderson.
But when I am asked what would keep my
spirits up in time for the hell and high water
that is waiting for care in the ER, I bop my
head side to side and motion for the radio to
turn up. *I got some things to get off my chest.*

American Horror Story: Racist Hospital Edition

they tell us
the hospital is a skeleton on the weekend
the doctor
is missing for hours
the oncologist
is missing for hours
they tell us
the hospital is a skeleton on the weekend
i tell 'em
i didn't plan to have this emergency
but next time i will know to schedule it

the nurse
wakes me in the early morning
jabs a needle like a dart into my vein
i ask groggily to use the bathroom
but she looks at me as we both
watch my maroon ink leak into tubes
i've already lost consent
meaning my voice can't forge
itself into anything

Stevie asks the nurses' station for
more water, food, and to flush my IV
every eight hours the nurses roll their eyes
inconvenienced by us knowing patient rights

or things only the doctors should know . . .
not us negroes but i been ready for this wasteland
—amerikkka's best-kept horror story:
the fermenting of patients' bodies

recipe: negligence
1 code blue and 1 technician
monitoring an entire floor
will ring the alarm a pinch too late
1 stampede of nurses galloping
down the hallway
let the body go stiff
prepare it to rest on a cot
serve the body to the freezer
place it next to the elderly woman
we locked in there alive
on accident

like we said
the hospital is a skeleton on the weekend
it needs your flesh and fat

"Lawsuit: Woman frozen alive in L.A. hospital died trying to escape."
LA Times, 2014

Medical Apartheid: A white boy says, *"Saw you post some heavy shit, hope you're doing okay"*

Inspired by "Karma" by Dominique Christina &
"Medical Apartheid" by Harriet A. Washington

The heavy "shit" is a Black disabled person dying.

The "shit" is a human being.
I am not okay, and I become less okay
when *shit* is the word coming out
an ivory-gated trap—a white boy who
don't know what it means to have a
lineage murdered because of hospitals.

He don't know medical neglect.
In fact, boy knows the *good doctor.*
The good doctor sits at the head of the
family table for dinner. Boy ain't seen
a doctor open up a black body bag for
yo Black ass to step into and that be the
expiration date assigned to us.
It ain't heavy "shit,"
it's a massacre.

It's medical apartheid.
It's experimentation to justify our enslavement.
It's Thomas Jefferson's legacy of injecting
200 enslaved Africans with cowpox.

Or James Marion Sims lauded
as the "Father of Modern Gynecology."
It's his experimentation as torture.
11 women, for 4 years, forced
to hold one another down during surgery,
coaxed into a dependency on opium
and morphine so "Father" could keep
Anarcha, Betsy, Lucy, and 'em in line.

It's medical schools competing with
one another over how many Black dead
people future doctors could dissect.
Violation after violation. Hold up
a cadaver to snap photos. Those porcelain
smiles gleaming on camera just like
they were doing with lynchings.

It's Tuskegee and withholding the cure.
It's withholding the cure to prove Black
people as a "syphilis-soaked race."
It's experimentation now justifying policy.
Justifying abuse of those incarcerated
and seeing them as "acres of skin"
and not people who they claim have
"volunteered" to be tested on.
But what is consent
when you are in prison to begin with?
When you need that money for commissary
and it ain't comin' from no place else?

It's eugenics and the Negro Project.

Margaret Sanger holding the birth control pill as legacy
—it's sterilization as population control,
as another violation where we cannot create legacy,
and it's real interestin' how it's the white folks
who got legacy to trace in this poem while our legacy
includes Black folks' bones littered underneath institutions.

It's the 1992 Columbia study.
Trying to prove Black kids as violent.
It's inaccurate studies so Hillary Clinton
can sit up and call us "superpredators."
It's Joe Biden's crime bill and Trump
pushing the wrongful conviction of the Central Park Five.
You see the way in which this ain't a system that's meant
    to protect us?
Care for us? Do anything on behalf of us?
The same government that chooses ignorance
when it comes to anything that isn't protecting
a cishet white man. It's Project Coast, it's MKNAOMI,
it's how AIDS became the disease of "those dirty niggas,"
the undesirables, the ones society tells us we should not
miss when they are gone. It's believing we don't feel pain.
Because they so used to us being dead that when we alive,
they don't even see us as such. We are not human. At times,
I question if I want to be human by this country's standards.
We deserve self-actualization, the space and place to do so,
to look at our own bodies and know they are not owned
by capitalism's billionaires, to not be prodded, tortured,
or stuffed away. This is the Black condition, so don't

disrespect us and refer to one of our own dying as "shit"
—see how even in death, you can't acknowledge a young
Black **person** is gone and your white ass can't respect us.
But go ahead, turn up your—I mean our—music.
Sit at your nice dining table in a condo in a Gotham-
Lookin' city and bop yo head to it. Forgettin' how history
repeats itself. You are a spectator, our life a battle royale.
Holding us in your phone like a snow globe.
Too enchanted with our culture to realize
there are cremated ashes fallin' out the bottom.

I Don't Need My Mother Before
She Needs Me Anymore

When I'm admitted to White Memorial Hospital with an infection and a white blood cell count of 200,000, Ivie's mother asks over the phone, *"Do you want to call your mom?"*
"No," I quip.

Again, I am bound to a hospital bed needing my damn mother's help before she needs mine. Stevie asks me, *"Are you sure you don't want to call her?"*
I shake my head and bat away tears.
"If it gets worse, I'll call her, but it won't need to get that far."

The next few days, I do my mother's job—crawl up the asses of everyone around me who wants to deny me care. I take notes when the doctors come in, ask the same questions she would, and for printouts of my labs. I remind my nurses of what they need to do, get up and walk around my room each day, ask for my gown and bedding to be changed, wash myself, eat my food, comb my hair, brush my teeth. I parent myself, meaning I love myself in the way I deserve to.

My friends take shifts watching over me. They bring me food, water, buy things at Target while on FaceTime, go downstairs to sneak in delivery food because . . . this hospital room's food is Styrofoam. They watch movies with me, comfort me in my panic attacks and crying spells, advocate for me when doctors shut me down, and help me tie together the back of my dainty blue gown. After almost seven days, we have inside jokes about hospital codes and my friends become more than my friends. They become my family.

My first hospital stay was a closure of sorts. I found out it was possible for my parents to extend the love I needed and it was possible for me to receive it, even if it was for a moment. I often let their leaving, their abuse, their own insecurities dictate how I feel about myself and those around me.

I've spent years believing "if my own mom cannot love me through cancer, nobody will," but now I have more empathy for her. She was close to my age when she first got diagnosed with her chronic illness. It interrupted her life the same way any chronic condition affects a young adult. Your twenties, your formative years, just aren't the same. You are left to explain your condition and limitations to people who don't understand and frankly don't want to. You find yourself wanting to be who you were before your illness. My mom always tried to rush me on from my cancer, to pretend it didn't exist in the same way I imagine she was told to move on from her diagnosis as if it did not exist. She did not want me to rest, and she hated when I talked about the diagnosis— especially when I talked about the politics of medical racism and cancer. Rage is a deep well that gives way to a prison of mourning.

On the third day at White Memorial, I look at the bottom of a well and see my mother. Her refusal to unpack it all. She did art once too. Bejeweling, miniature dollhouses, anything with your hands, really. My grandaddy scoffed at the lack of stability for a profession. But something in medicine, *people are always going to need that.* But she wanted to be an artist, like me. Of all people,

I thought she'd understand me being a poet, but she denied me the same agency that she was denied. I am sad for the ways her father did not allow her to just be. At White Memorial, I am presented with a choice—a rarity in illness. Am I going to let my cancer tell me I am undeserving of support and love and life? Or am I going to say *to hell with it, I am entitled to my own healing.* I choose the second option. I choose the second option and choose not to call her. I call on *her* mother's spirit instead.

I am handed my advanced directive and look to my left side for my mother, like I did back in April 2017. But she ain't here. It's me, alone. This time, I'm the one who writes what I want done to preserve my life and end it. I choose what I want for myself without seeking her approval. If I die, it's on my terms. If I live, it's on my terms. And the time in-between, I resolve to love on my terms as well. That's not to say the shit doesn't hurt, but love has always been what has kept me here, what has saved me. Even my mother's for just those seven days in a hospital in 2017.

When I am wheeled out of White Memorial after five days, waiting in the parking lot for a friend to pull their car around, I feel the breeze for the first time in a week and rub my hands on my legs, thinking to myself: *I did that shit. I need me for my damn self.* The nurse beside me interrupts my moment and asks, *"Where's your family?"* And I know the nurse was more so frustrated about why my friend was taking so long to show up with her car, but I take it differently, and my heart doesn't hurt either way.

"They're on the way."

I Keep Choking on You in My Sleep

A gun crawls its way out of a drain.
The chamber releases itself.
The drain is my mouth,
and my partner's brains
are on the floor. The floor,
littered with bullets.
Hundreds of rounds mocking me.

A PICC line sucks itself into my veins.
My heart rattles with metal.
The doctors say
there is nothing they can do,
and I yell for my family.
No one can hear me
when I choke on a sauna of sweat.

My clothes do not live in the closet anymore.
Last time my body was inside,
I was snatching a gun from my partner
and she cried of rotting from the inside.

The closet is a dungeon of spoiled meat.
It reeks, and I have lost track of how many
ceremonies I've done to forget.

Trauma is the parasite.

I am waking and hollow
and eight years old,
hiding under the covers, hoping
my mother's spite will forget how to find me.
That my father's hands will lose track of me.
Abuse is their idea of parenting,
and I'm little me lost in a maze.

A record of my mother
calling me bad and stupid
plays on the loudspeakers.
I sit in a corner, hiding inside my arms.
Remembering my mother
grabbing me by the hair in third grade
and swinging my head around.
God, I had hoped she'd snap my neck already,
but I am forever her faulty wishbone.
Lying awake cuz I can't suffocate
on the price of dreaming.
Two hawks circle my home.
A butterfly rests at the window.
I can't remember a day
when I have not recycled
Pluto's extremes.

The Breakdown I Can Only Dream to Have

I want to break down:
a *click-click-boom*
and I'm a tornado
flinging responsibility
from my body.
I want to be an absolute disaster:
let my throat unchain itself
& kindly say piss off to the
next person who tries me.
I am not made to carry
all the world's matter.
Won't wait for anyone
to allow my refusal.
I am unbuckling
my knees because
I will not carry
everyone else's sad.
Let a scream rip like
a champagne bottle popping
then change my name
& move to a different country.
Better yet, Imma unload you
and your problems from my back
and throw them to the side like
extra baggage I am finished
with carrying you all's impossible

expectations Want me like a
circus animal Press fast-forward
and in two seconds, I will finally
let myself be a rabid beast
frothing at the jaws
screaming and running
directionless, but no one
is demanding labor from me:
the work mule, the teacher,
the therapist, the strong one,
your inspirational story,
career advisor, & keeper of time.
Never mind me when I whisper,
"Give me a break"
Never mind me when I cry
I can't keep doing this
I guess I'm just dramatic
So I plan to be the whole
damn theater house
showing a new play
It will be called:
A Black Person Rests.
I will be a calm calamity
The most beautiful
strike of lightning
because I gave myself
permission to be electric.
And then I will sleep
until I am forgotten
because sometimes

I just don't want
to be perceived.
Goodness, I am weak,
I am a fragile thing
with a temper like
California in August.
I want to sink into myself
knowing I belong to myself
That I am not the property
of some stranger's expectations
or the angel of a selfish demon
What a mess I plan to be
—such a glorious surrender
to no longer be responsible
for everyone else's self-imploding.

7 Layers of Post-Traumatic Stress Disorder
(After "7 Layers of Hell" by Sierra DeMulder)

the first layer
is the back seat of a Nissan Pathfinder.
My mother
cannot contain grief
& the car is filled with
the black smoke of funeral clothes.
She says, *"I can't do this"* with panic

until

her eyes glaze over
and
I am the one forced to speak
to Death on behalf of my family.

My mother's mother
ascended two weeks before,
meaning I lost the only mother I ever knew too.

My spirit leaves me while "Somewhere
Over the Rainbow" plays to a casket
dressed in vermin—in this layer,
my soul is murdered one thousand times
over & thirteen is adulthood.

the second layer
is every man I have been too afraid
to say no to gathering in my childhood bedroom.
Their drunken fists and predatory lust contort
my home into an escape room—
a threatening riddle made of their manhood.

Here, I discover the darkest magic,
how to sever my head from my body
if it means I survive to be silent tomorrow.

the third layer
is eight years old & my mother
tying my hair around her wrists &
pendulum-swinging my head
like abuse is a meditative practice.

the fourth layer
is the psychiatrist
with a room full of crystals
overlooking Beverly Hills.
He likens me to a combat veteran.
My therapist chimes in, calling
my life a documentary on
psychological torture,
tied to a chair.
The past & present convene
to force-feed me prescriptions.

the fifth layer
is the night before the cancer diagnosis.
The world spins off its axis—but only to me.
I stumble down the stairs. Every oxygen particle
escapes the room cackling. The next day, I am dying
and the hospital wants me dead too. The doctors use
a needle to drill a hole into my back to find the cancer,
a wound that never unlearns its bleeding.

In this room, those twelve hours repeat,
I scream & no one hears a thing.

the sixth layer
is me standing outside my home,
looking in through a window.
My partner is texting love notes
to a white woman from our bed
while holding a gun with her free hand.
I ask for love through the glass, and
she runs to the closet. I shatter.
My partner lives but my body fails me again.

the seventh layer
is me at four or five years old.
A man holding my hand.
Pandora's box rattles.
I question reality,
and I become my abusers.

Gaslight myself into oblivion.
Make it so I never existed
& become nothing
but
a myth.

I Meet My Psychiatrist for the First Time and the Color Theory behind Red Forms

I wring my hands together anxiously in the Uber driving me to Beverly Hills. The Westside. The side of town for the rich people of Los Angeles. I am not here to shop on Rodeo Drive or find a celebrity to stop. No, today I get to tell a complete stranger what my therapist suspects: I am mentally ill. As hell.

I am let out of the Uber in front of Blue Bottle Coffee, and I roll my eyes as I remember how they were gentrifying Downtown LA years ago. This is the fancy side of town where your nonfat skinny latte with oat milk on the side will cost as much as someone else's groceries for the day.

I walk across a concrete plaza where white-collar businessmen take their "very important" phone calls, and I am: Black, young, tatted, in black leggings that are not Lululemon, a black shirt with flames, and Dr. Martens that make me tower at six feet tall. I stick out—not in a good way. People like me ain't supposed to be on this side of town.

I shuffle my feet into my psychiatrist's office building. I wave at security, skip into the next elevator available. I tiptoe down the hallway and push open a heavy door. Enter a burgundy waiting room. Dark, with a warm yellow light. In many ways, this place feels more like an empty lounge at a velvet supper club where the jazz band is preparing their next set.

Dr. Weisberg greets me and lets me into yet another office. Intricate art nailed to the walls; every crystal I can think of and ones I don't know are scattered across his chunky, beautifully carved office desk. I have three options when it comes to where I want to sit, so Hypervigilance chooses the couch near the door in case I need a quick exit.

"So tell me what's going on," he asks.

Dr. Weisberg is a somewhat tall, lanky white man with platinum white hair. He has an air of authority that makes me feel comfortable. I can tell it's not to make me feel insignificant but rather for me to feel secure. Like he knows what he is doing. I bite my lip. Trying to not let all the symptoms show I am a working mess.

I relay the past nights, waking up from nightmares about being experimented on in hospitals and screaming while being torn apart from family. I think it's a generational pain. I've been choking when I wake up because my partner just tried to end her life when I tried to leave. Sometimes I'm convinced it's a hook lodged inside my shoulder and that's why I'm hurting from being reeled out of my element. My heart acts like my namesake, beating as quickly as a hummingbird's wings when I'm nervous. I am a very nervous person.

Uncertainty sort of does that, but then there are times when I'm Atlas and the weight of the world is on my shoulders and femurs break through my skin and I fall apart. Falling apart is feeling suicidal. It's this fizzing as the shower water runs over my head.

"Do it, no one will miss you," or *"There's too many barriers anyway, so be the ruler of your own universe and disappear."* I repeat, *"Then is not now"* until my memories stop tryna jump me.

Concentration is—sorry, what were we talking about? Right, symptoms. I feel like I'm suffering; I don't deserve suffering, at least I think I don't. I rattle on about symptoms from childhood to adulthood: What remained consistent. Who stayed absent. What I've gone through, what I'm going through.

He likens me to Job from the Bible, a man faced with impossible tasks, whose steady faith kept him alive. I think faith and hope are the only two things that keep me alive. He talks me through what he thinks might be going on: depression, anxiety, PTSD, and ADHD. A diagnosis provides relief. *I'm not meant to live like this; there is something better.* He offers his thoughts on what prescription medication would be best. "Now, we're going to start slow; it may take a few weeks to see or feel a difference. If you feel anything is wrong, do not hesitate to call me," he says gently, with warm eyes shining behind his spectacles.

I know Black folks don't trust the medical system, and I don't trust it all that much either. I also know how many times I have been told that what is happening in my brain is not real. It's cultural for us, and I get it: We want to solve these things ourselves if that means less contact with the system. Therapy and psychiatry are "white people shit," and it is "white people shit" because therapists and psychiatrists are more accessible for white people to utilize. I look to the right, and Dr. Weisberg's window is showing me how much open space exists, and perhaps that's a metaphor or signal for me to understand. How do I make space or take space for myself to expand? I look down at the prescription written for me. The pills aren't the cure; they are the aids, a symbol of my willingness to try everything I can to just stay: here.

You Ask Me Why I Still Want You
Since You've Hurt Me Over and Over

When you almost die, it drives home there is always
    time for redemption.
Our hearts remain our greatest weapon. I am a coin flip
    depending on the day.
Two-sided: jaded and optimistic. I want us to transcend
    this critical need
to exonerate ourselves from pride, and instead we can say,
    "I'm sorry,"
"I'm going to commit to doing better," and actually mean it.

I believe in us just like the night I stood in a black-lace crop top
and a black skirt with short, curly black hair. I looked
    like a funeral,
but I did a poem outside of City Hall, one that I wrote earlier
    in the day,
watching you cooking eggs for our breakfast. I still got it in
    our memory box.
That night, I jumped into your arms when you said, *"I think
    I love you."*
I had never felt more special in my life. A few hours later,
I said, *"I think I love you?"* with a red heart-shaped lamp
    beating in the corner.
Never had this feeling been reciprocated.

Love is redemption. So let us nurture ourselves again.
We cannot be past the nights in DC when we would walk
for miles with each other just to get to your school or my job
or the room I was renting. We walked everywhere together,
would split Utz chips and Little Debbies for dinner,
counting quarters at the bus stop in the morning, and laughter
was all we needed even while leukemia watercolored bruises
    on my thighs.

We sang "Come What May" and "No Day but Today."
We both desperately didn't want something to be wrong.
Circumstances have changed us, but I see us as so precious
and worth saving. Been riding for you three years and not even
cancer could separate us. Until it could. I hate myself for ruining
anything good. I promise I'll try to get better soon. I don't know
how, but I'll sit in a scatter of red carnations like the ones you
bought in a red Che Guevara shirt to match.
    I will strum Paramore's
"All I Wanted" on my mint Fender, waiting for you to fill
    in the chorus.
Only if you want this too.

Change = Grief + Acceptance

I read an essay to my therapist today. He thanks me for writing it, and we muse on change. How cancer seems to demand us and everyone around us to change constantly whether we are ready for it or not. We discuss if that change is not addressed properly, then perhaps it can lead to deep resentment and imbalance. I tell him it's hard to not let my cancer essentialize me, to not say, *"Cancer makes me a bad thing,"* *"Well, this wouldn't happen if I didn't have cancer."*

He gives a small smirk and strokes his beard. *"Yes, I remember one of our first sessions together, I had you draw where your cancer was in relation to yourself.*

"It was this black thing in your heart with tentacles almost taking you over."

"Yeah, I forget it's not that. I'm trying to remember my body is an ecosystem."

"Right, the cancer can be the marsh, but there are mountains, there's grass, there are rivers, and the marsh isn't inherently bad . . . it's just there."

My therapist proceeds to ask me if I've heard of different schools of psychology, as he takes out a notepad and draws a stick figure.

"See, usually when there's a person who says to an audience, 'Do you want change?' The audience yells, 'Yes!!!'" He draws a ton of exclamation points.

He draws another stick figure. "Now, if that same person then asks, 'Do you want to change?' The audience drifts off with, "Eh?" He draws a bunch of question marks.

He then draws the last stick figure. "And if that same person asks, 'Do you want to lead change?' The whole audience will just dash out of the room." He draws a series of dashes.

It's important to identify that change is needed, change is necessary, then ask: Do we want to commit to doing the work in order to change ourselves, to brave the unknown within ourselves?

My therapist then makes a point. "Most people think change is to accept things that are transforming, but in actuality, change is to accept reality as is." He then pulls out his pad again and writes: **Change = Grief + Acceptance**. And that's when my therapist writes out the acronym for *Mourn The Person We Could've Been*.

According to the formula above, it's also not my responsibility to reconcile people's ideas of who I should've been and who I should be pre- and post-diagnosis. Over the phone, my white grandmother, the one I hardly talk to, the one who I resent because my grandma and granny are not here, the one who always says something offensive "accidentally," because it's just the "German" thing to do, sighs in a high-pitched voice. "You know, [insert dead name], we had such high hopes for you. You were at NYU, you were going to be a doctor, and now look at you, a college dropout with cancer." Shame comes and chloroforms me. I was her investment too. I am bad luck at the casino because I am not who everyone in my life decides for me. But I still am pining for their affections, doing everything possible to find a way to go back to being the poet I was, the fiancée I was, the collegiate student I was, the worker I was, and each time, my body surrendered and my illness took charge to say, *"Give this shit up."*

When I'm able to hear my own voice, it seethes with rage: Look at you now? What does that even mean? Yeah, take it all in, I'm a college dropout with cancer . . . still living? Does that make me pitiful? It's a funeral in an office on North La Brea at 10:30 a.m., open casket, chapel has room for two: my therapist and me.

"A funeral is meant to be a celebration for what is dead to influence what still lives, so do that." twenty-three-year-old *me stands at the pulpit and yells,* **"This ain't your eulogy; you are bearing witness to a past self's death, slither out your skin like a snake in the Garden of Eden. If being yourself is a bad thing, then return the fruit to them, let them be naked in their ignorance. Wandering."**

"The only lasting truth is Change. God Is Change."

—*Octavia E. Butler,* **Parable of the Sower**

Invisible Heavenly Bodies

Place white cloth over your head.
Wear white down to your feet.
Prepare the camphor in the black cauldron.
Grab the holy water. Open a window
and wash the floor with Kananga water.

Lay down white lace and light two white candles.
Let the flames flick—see the smoke twirl.
Turn from dolphin to snake to wolf.

Speak the prayers with closed
eyes and pressed palms. Whisper
a Bible verse or a psalm. Meet an
ancestor at a dock by a blue bay
like Otis Redding said. Or meet
in the middle of a beaten path,
the thick of Jasper, Texas, woods,
or while pedaling to keep head
above water with your ankles
tied to the ocean floor.

Roll the dice and always see
4, 7, or 10. Prepare the offerings:
Crown Royal, rum, Dr Pepper,
tomato soup, chocolate bars, chili,
a bouquet of flowers, tobacco,

red beans and rice, gumbo, chips.
Honey, we can keep going, but
keep the water clear, never dirty.

Adore the photos of family members smiling.
Each one has their own photo with their own corner.
Make it comfortable for them.
They are not gone, I promise you.
They are here in a way that requires faith.

So call in the ancestors whose names you do know.
Shuffle the deck of ole-school playing cards and
somehow the Ace of Spades stays following you.

Make the mojo bag. Keep it wrapped tight to you.
Boil the bath. Organize the herbs. Move the lodestones
and High John the Conqueror. Flick Hoyt's Cologne.

You, the child of seers.
Don't ignore the dreams
or the intuition or the times
this pen is feelin' like it's got a will of its own,
that another being's hand is guiding your own,
let the message still be delivered—it is meant for you.

When the droning doctor asks in 2017
as you are dying slowly in a hospital bed
how long ago was the last time you've had a physical.
You will learn this cancer has been here for
a long time, most likely before 2015, and

has been playing a soft symphony until it
became a cacophony of noisy white blood cells.

Do not absolve yourself of your worst moments.
Guilty hands, flighty feet, and a tongue that
can both heal and manipulate. Lean into
knowing and understanding the pain
you've caused others. Lean into compassion,
for this is not a punishment or a karmic debt.
Everything will be revealed like a curtain call.
I know it's overwhelming, but

Be open, stay observant
Be soft, stay sharp
Be realistic, stay dreaming
Be childlike, stay wise
Be pure, stay unholy
Be holy, stay a sinner
Be principled, sharpen the blade

Go to the water.
Big Mama. Yemaya. Olokun.
Give your offerings. Wade out
knee-deep to watch her swallow
everything but you.

It takes work to be here.

Keep lighting the candles so
your people can find you.

You the only one with an altar,
so when the family is present,
they fill an entire room: Mary, Jennie, Dave,
Susan, Genevieve, Alberta, Dave, Jennie,
Ike, Pearl, Gerald, Walter, Sissie, Hallie, Richard,
Raymond, Harriet, Patsy, George, Robert,
Adeline, Lark, Billie, and all the family members
who are but a number and their names will forever
go unspoken consequently.

Watch for the monarch butterflies,
welcome the hawks,
don't startle the hummingbirds.
They all follow you with reason.
You were made for this.

Wear Grandaddy's gold medallion with his cursive initials.
Wear Grandma's gold-chain bracelet on your left wrist.
Wear Granny's elephant ring hugging your left ring finger.

You are protected in a realm where there are more forces
beyond your kin keeping you here, so thank God, thank Spirit,
thank your guides, thank those who have come to visit you
momentarily.

Move slow and with intention. Play Billie Holiday,
Etta James, Bessie, Al Green, Donny Hathaway,
Charlie Parker, The Whispers and The Spinners,
Luther Vandross, Ray Charles, Robert Johnson,

Chuck Berry, Memphis Minnie, Big Lucky Carter,
Bo Diddley, Junior Wells, Jelly Jaw Short,
Screamin' Jay Hawkins, Champion Jack Dupree.

Dance alongside your family.
Cook a feast alongside your family.
Talk to them while watching your favorite shows.
Gossip. Fall to the ground in pain. Sit beside your family
before the day knows to begin. Take it in, all of you,
invisible heavenly bodies.

"Why did you go through with a stem cell transplant?"
"Because I didn't want to spend the rest of my life wondering what could've happened."

—*Kathryn Poe*

"I feel like choosing to get a lung transplant, for me, means to experience a lot of pain and trusting you're going to do something worthwhile, and I don't think I've been myself for a long time, but I'm starting to."

—*Claire Wineland*

I . . . Think I Wanna Look in to Doing a Stem Cell Transplant?

Stem cell transplant has always been the nail in the coffin.
It's been the "you only do that when things get *really* bad."
So what if I don't want to *wait* for things to get really bad
when they already started off really bad.
Heard that only 23 percent of Black patients find matches
who can donate that new immune system, that second ticket at life.
I'm no good at math, but I do understand how finite time is.
"Things getting really bad" could be next week
or two or five years from now.
More than anything, I want to be responsible to myself.
So how neglectful would it be to ignore that cancer
does not care for the boundary setting
I learned in therapy last week?
I've been watching YouTube videos,
and I've been talking to patients,
and I want to think I can do it.
I want to believe I deserve
more than waiting.

Understanding Requires Discipline

Robin Roberts is the only Black person
with a national platform
who had a stem cell transplant
and documented it.

Her body was beaten down by chemotherapy,
but she's still steady, determined.
Walks with a decorated IV pole
on *Good Morning America*
and still lives. To this day.

Sharing our stories is not rooted
solely in tragedy or inspiration.
It's to put the others up on game.
Others. Like me.
She taps her fingernails
against my laptop screen,
a warning:
This will not be easy,
prepare for the unthinkable,
make peace with the possible.

Her videos,
the guide entitled:
"If You Really Want This,
Go and Get It.
Without a Single
Apology to Anyone."

Pinafore St

Thirty units and our new neighbor, Frank, sits up in faded overalls and claims we got the best apartment on the property. We live in the Jungles now, across the way from an elementary school. Kids clog the street with faint, excited screams at recess as we move our first pieces of "adult" IKEA furniture from the truck rental. A TV stand; a bookcase near identical to the one from my childhood home; a white shag rug, a circular glass coffee table; an extendable dining room table with cushioned chairs; more cookware for Taco Tuesdays, pasta, curries, salmon, and the inevitable Postmates order to be reheated.

We've never had this much space: eight hundred square feet of gray paneled flooring, three closets, a popcorn ceiling, double doors for double safety. We pinch ourselves when I brew coffee in an aqua-blue mini Keurig machine for the two of us, and we sip out of matching mugs.

In the mornings, we walk hand in hand and take Riley on walks around the neighborhood. Wave to the older Black folks sitting on their stoops or waiting for the bus. This was all I ever wanted as a child. It may be three years later than *we* wanted, but we have our own home with a welcome mat. A denim couch is where we fall asleep on each other before groggily stumbling into the bedroom and under lilac comforters.

"Even with cancer, you always got us, baby," Ivie whispers into my neck.

I'm still not over what has happened in the past. I heard it takes two years to recover from betrayal trauma. Maybe here, I can forget. No one has died here, no ghosts stand over our bed, we are alone. A trial run for this family thing, this love thing, this everything thing, a second chance to really do this almost-marriage thing right. I got an ivory dress hanging up that I like to envision a wedding in sometimes. Short with a plunging V-neck and white Steve Madden heels to match. Ivie holds me from behind and gives me a slight squeeze. Asks when we're gonna go to the Beverly Hills Courthouse and make our marriage official to the state. Hoping honesty bodes well, I say, *"Soon."*

Life Decisions Made in the Bathroom
of Bossa Nova Brazilian Cuisine

Date night is at the Brazilian spot down the street from the Landmark—a bougie movie theater I worked at five years ago. The Manuella's pasta was split between coworkers in the locker room. Stuffing mouthfuls into our faces between ripping tickets, sweeping theaters, checking on audiences during movies, and helping whatever rich white person who felt personally slighted by choosing a movie they didn't like.

I did not expect to be back here. With a fiancée this far removed from 2014, riding the #7 Big Blue to and from work, drinking with coworkers, smoking in the carpools home, detours to food trucks like Leo's Tacos and neighborhoods covered in Christmas lights. I was invincible back then. Things change, but my order hasn't. Cooks are boiling the pasta, sauteing the shrimp, prepping the herbs, shouting among one another just within earshot. I excuse myself and go to the bathroom.

Bounce my knee on the toilet, waiting for Instagram to load. I have spent the day asking stem cell transplant patients why they ultimately went through with something this uncertain. Kathryn's is the bold message at the top of my inbox. Unread. Blinking. They had made a photo diary to show people like me what their transplant and ongoing recovery were actually like. They weren't pretty. Again, what about chronic illness and the treatment is supposed to be beautiful?

"I didn't want to spend the rest of my life wondering what would have happened if I went through transplant," Kathryn replies.

A part of me was searching for answers to scare me away from decision-making. There was another part that needed to find someone to write what I already knew: I don't want to spend the rest of my life wondering what could have happened. I don't want a preventable death. I don't want to wait until the final call and have my body decide nothing is going to work.

Mascara pools in my tear ducts. I stride out to a dimmer-lit restaurant. Return to my seat and hold Ivie's hands across the large table. Our pasta in large white bowls, already delivered, steaming with the long-lost promise that to be young is to be untouchable. I know the difference now.

"I'm gonna follow through with this transplant. It's not going to be easy, but it's going to be worthwhile." Freeing one hand, I twirl pasta around my fork, not waiting for anyone's response to validate my self-preservation.

The Lyft driver stops at a red light
before turning into the driveway
guiding cars to City of Hope's
fountain and valet—"Is this—
is this a cancer hospital?"
"Yeah, it's my first time here."
"They saved my aunt's life here.
This a good place, a real good place,
good people too."
—telephone is Black people tellin'
each other which hospitals won't kill us

Journal Entry: My Last Cancer Support Group Meeting in Person until Next Time, Oct. 2019

Prompt: Two of the most common metaphors are 'battle' and 'journey' for the experience of illness. How, if at all, do you relate?

I'm sitting in therapy, and I tell my therapist about the difference three years has made with this illness. I say I felt like I was in the back seat of a car, and I don't know who's driving, but someone is, and I know at the end, we are going to meet this impending doom. The day I chose to pursue a transplant was me clamoring into the front, hitting the brakes, and busting a doughnut—dangerous, but at least I knew where I wanted to go.

My therapist tells me this is self-realization—something I was denied for years, even before my cancer. That part is the journey—elated I get to practice some autonomy but also crying because no one should ever have to make decisions like this.

The journey means that no matter what choice we do or don't make, there will still be crossroads. A busted gasket. Who the hell knows. And I'm trying to learn to just cruise through, you know? I promise I am really just tryna focus on what's directly in front of me. But there's this nagging voice that asks, *"What if December 2019 is your last Christmas?" "What if February 2020 is your last birthday?" "What will happen to Ivie if you die?" "Are you happy with how you lived?"*

So just cruising doesn't work either. That's like being in the back seat except I am only lightly gripping the wheel. Truth is, the journey is learning to balance the contradictions. Standing on one foot with this planet off its axis, asking whatever being up in the sky to cut you some slack. The journey is: Cancer has been the worst thing that ever happened to me.

The journey is: Cancer somehow was the best thing that ever happened to me.

If not for leukemia, I would have never given myself the permission to survive on my own terms. The journey is the contradiction of being infuriated and thankful.

It's looking at how my cancer wants to kill me, and how I was almost okay with that.

Spent so many years suicidal, cancer was a more honorable death than suicide.

At least then the tombstone will read, WALELA TRIED: A FALLEN ANGEL as opposed to WALELA FLIPPED OFF THE WORLD. It's all about acknowledging the irony that in some ways,

my cancer saved me, because did you know it is actually really so fucking terrifying being invested in living?

I'm just trying to make it through living on this highway alongside everyone else. That is the most I can really ask for. The battle is the trauma, the journey is the acceptance, and I'm frozen in the middle tryna do better in both.

I Dropped Out of College After My First Semester, But . . .

I prepare to present my dissertation.

Fourteen pages on "why you should give a damn,"

also known as "I need a stem cell transplant,"

also known as "Medi-Cal patients get

the short end of the stick, so listen up,"

also known as "I can speak your language too,

see: graphs and charts on pages seven through ten.

I've been watching conferences you probably attended,

so 'no' ain't an answer I am accepting."

City of Hope is already different

than any place I've been treated.

The staff are . . . nice?

They care that I'm . . . nervous?

I sit in an examination chair.

Shifting my body, anticipating—

The oncologist enters: balding, closer to my height,

and on his white coat, a collection of Disney lapel pins like

the ones I used to collect as a child.

He is not like the others. He's a grandfather to somebody,

    I can tell.

He asks for my handiwork and flips through each page.

Reading. Indulging the concept that maybe I do

know what I am talking about. I wring my knuckles,

waiting for him to challenge me about point five on page

seven or the conclusion on page fourteen. This is more
than a dissertation;
I prep for the inevitable cross-examination these doctors do.
He adjusts the half-moon spectacles on the bridge of his nose.
"You know, you likely won't be able to have your own children,"
he cautions.
"Great, good thing I don't want any," I snap back with my
white-girl smile.
Raise my eyebrows to indicate, *"Yeah, buddy, I got an answer
for everything too."*
Been in so many offices where being defensive was the difference
between being heard or unheard, getting the authorization
I need for care or not.
He lets out a sigh and shuffles my papers together. I brace for
the absolute worst:
I wasted my time and money on overzealousness.
*"Mmhmm. Okay, I don't see why not.
We'll put in an order for testing."*

The Tests to Calculate If My Body
Can Withstand a Transplant

One orange jug of twenty-four-hour urine collection
that is wildly embarrassing to carry in an Uber.

One EKG and an investigation into
my heart chamber, observing
cardiac function.

One pulmonary test,
blowing into spirometers in
different breath patterns to measure
the health and inflation of two hot-air balloons.

A chest X-ray that casts a white shadow.
A CT scan to reveal what may be a cause
for worry, except it's a new scar.

Countless bloodwork orders
to observe my counts, if my kidney
and liver can indeed rid toxic waste,
and if there's exposure to infectious diseases.

Tests measuring where the leukemia is lying in wait.

A physical exam.

The genealogy of my family's health history.

A social-worker-and-psychologist evaluation.

How do you
feel about
transplant?
Anything
coming up?

I chose this,
so,
Confident.

I Didn't Know My Last Christmas Would Be My Last Because of Miss Rona

Stevie comes over to decorate Oreo-and-gumdrop gingerbread houses from Michaels. We put up the fake Christmas tree with Ivie, weaving rainbow lights through green plastic tree branches and topping it off with a gold star. I spend ten minutes strategically placing a heavy silver ornament in the middle. It has a red door, a green wreath, and an "Our First Christmas" banner with the year: 2020. Our first apartment in the Jungles is the epicenter of my first real Christmas in four years. Traditions I created in solitude, I allow others to see. I stand over the apartment's white stove, melting Ghirardelli milk chocolate chips. Mix together crushed Oreos and cream cheese in a bowl, pat them into round truffles for the chocolate to coat. Open the fridge and clear out the middle shelf for them to be chilled into no-bake cheesecake truffles. Let them sit for an hour and some change before serving. TLC's "Sleigh Ride" plays out the Rokit speakers underneath a copy of Ernie Barnes's *Late Night DJ*—a Black woman with a red dress inside a radio booth, holding a vinyl record to play. None of us thought we would ever make it this far still intact, even partially, but we did, and we gettin' grown with it now. Ivie is in school and working part-time, I'm working full-time booking workshops at colleges on ableism and racism, Stevie is working full-time at a school. We done come a long way from Starbucks. We pour eggnog out of glass bottles from Bristol Farms like I used to do at my parents' house. A wreath decorates our front door with fake poinsettias and pine cones. Stockings for Ivie and me: a plush

Santa and a plush snowman. A Black Santa figurine sits at the centerfold of our dark brown Ikea dining table with a handcrafted pine cone arrangement. I place a mini emerald frosted tree with tiny metallic presents next to Santa, and fill up our matching porcelain Frosty the Snowman mugs with hot chocolate. We watch *Krampus* and ABC Claymation movies and fall asleep in the living room. Maturity cementing into a family tradition.

Journal Entry: COVID Got Me Fucked Up: March 2020

In Target, people prepare for a global health pandemic concerning a deadly airborne virus by hoarding toilet paper, Lysol spray, hand sanitizer, bottled water. Coughing on people wearing masks because the CDC hasn't told them yet to be wearing them like I am.

The store is rattling with the sound of people fast-walking in a frenzy—lookin' for anything to scapegoat is what people choose to hold on to—the *"you don't need to wear a mask," "you're too extra with that."* Yes, I am extra—look at me strut around, for I was wearing a mask before your world was ending because mine started ending in 2017. April 10th. Diagnosis day. Almost-dead day. I don't roll the dice on my own life. I don't let nobody gamble with my tombstone no more. Been wearing a mask for twelve months now so I can go experience people or just the outside, like . . . doing things people normally do . . . like going to Target.

But people don't seem to want me here with their jokes and sudden paranoia that makes them lose all common sense. This ain't nothin' new. Seventy percent of the time there is a nervous shift when I enter an Uber or a restaurant; the drivers or store owners begin looking around frantically—waiting for me to do just enough of a scary thing so they can call the cops on me cuz a Black person with a mask is automatically a robbery. And they don't have to say it for that simple fact to be understood between us—to them, I walk into stores like I'm a cowboy:

"I'm a cancer patient and this is a stickup cuz I'm Black. Black
with a mask on—at some points, said mask is bedazzled. I got
my bright neon green braids down to my waist and here is my
left arm—a mural of tattoos. Yep, that's a Black Power fist. Oop, I
know knowing my own history is not supposed to be 'the negro's'
reality. That alone makes me one of the most easily identifiable
criminals in broad daylight. This is my gun. Wait, sorry, those are
my fingers. Also, this is my credit card because I'm tryna get to my
therapist, or I'm trying to go to pick up my salmon bowl and some
green juice to pretend healthy food is accessible. Yeah, man, you all
got me—I put the fear of the Devil in you for protecting my health.
You got me, buddy. Arrest me. People will do anything to make
themselves unacquainted with fear—even it means devaluation of
a stranger minding their damn business."

When the Oral Chemo Fails, Part Two: BOSULIF

If there is a different torture,
please, I welcome it.
Deluge my leukemia
in a poison to bring
my body back.
It's been hovering
on the ceiling
above me.
Boneless.
Skinless.
Eyeless.
Inside out.
I honor the horror
just enough to welcome it.
One shadow of many to return.

there will be more pandemics

The news reports of small towns
wiped out by the effects of globalization.

COVID will not be our first pandemic or our last.
Blame the right people:
no one other than elite corporations.
Slicing, drilling, extracting,
burning the Earth of her finite resources.

Capitalism is abusing nature,
and the animals (including us)
are migrating to higher ground.

We are not past the age of disease.
We are entering the era of preventable spread.

Money is power. We are hamsters
spinning on wheels trying to afford rent.
The cost of living is unlivable.
Amazing, in the "land of opportunity,"
we are all a paycheck away from ruin.

Mass Death & Productivity

Mass Death arrives, and Productivity asks us to pay it no mind.
It costs money to have empathy, to need sleep, but Productivity
needs us half-awake, army-crawling toward a dollar bill.
Mass Death is desensitizing everybody, and Productivity
thrives on the apathy and individualism and hustle/grind culture.
Productivity needs us to not care about one another because
then we don't need one another. Instead, we need it.
It. As in productivity. We need money. We need to get it
    on our own.
There is a way of doing this better.
Example: A friend bought me groceries, slid me a $100 bill,
and I cried yesterday. Other friends drop off prescriptions
and lists I send via text for groceries from the nearby Ralphs.
See, Productivity don't want you to even know your own neighbor.
A pandemic sprouts up one million tombstones.
The government tells us to keep on workin'.
But I don't want Productivity's name mentioned in my home
cuz that ain't nothin' but a myth, ain't nothing but an
    old wives' tale
written by capitalism: Capitalism needs a body to exploit? You?
Got a "healthy," able body? Then you got a nice landscape to mine.
Until you don't got any resources [labor] to give.
Go to the landfill and see just how quick you went from person
to worker to trash and you didn't even notice it.
You didn't even get to enjoy life—we've been taught to
    obey Mass Death

and Productivity as "ways of living"—the price of living
    under a government
that can fund wars and the military but
    not eradicate houselessness.
It's difficult for me to answer the question: What is Living, then?
In this economy? Does anybody have the answer for what it means
to be alive and not sell my body and morality for
    a company's profit?

To Be Young, Black, and Gay and Lonely

Audre said that first in the 1950s.
Now it's 2020.
There is a virus killing millions,
and plastic people fill my Instagram
from parties to celebrate this need
for social validation in a time
of death and disease.
I am not welcome.
The invitations never came.
Cancer is isolating enough.
Seeing "friends" hide gatherings
from me. To not make me feel. Bad.
To not make themselves feel. Bad.
Because. I am. Masked. Ill.
Queer. Black. And. Lonely.
There is little understanding.
Receiving consequences
for circumstances
outside my control.
No one knows where
to pinpoint the Hurt.
He's breathing inside me.
Our voices braided together.

The Codependent Waltzes to FKA Twigs's "Cellophane," Nov. 2020

I don't know when you stopped showing up or when I taught myself to stop noticing. One day, I thought I saw you disappear into a thousand black crows on Crenshaw, and I don't know who was left behind. She was glassy-eyed. I morphed myself into whatever was needed for you to love me. Even if it was for a moment. Even if you took care of me for only a couple hours, then that meant you were still in love with me. You still cared for me. But you were never there. You are a fractured, haunted being—a disappearing act.

Think. The appointments in which anxiety was a howling tunnel. I was coughing up blood in the waiting room, but you were busy on your phone. Mumbling on about how you don't know how to help. Hardly ever looking up from your screen. Paying attention to whoever made you think less about me and made you feel big about yourself. You did not at least try to clean up the mess. I know we are both young, and who lets two people navigate something as big as this alone? But we are here on a boat with bullet holes. I'm asking you to roll up your sleeves, fill the buckets, throw the excess water and baggage overboard. We are an excruciatingly slow sinking.

Your answer is nearly always no. Demand more from me. Never see the double standard I am held prisoner to. Baby, do you not hear me screeching in the morning about how tired I am? I have said for years I am so tired. Need I remind you that some of this is your job too; we chose a life together. If you don't want any of it, then say so.

You want to stay, allegedly. I ask you to share responsibility with me. You punch a wall. Stoicism becomes my middle name. I tend to myself only when you sleep and in the wee hours of morning. I do not want your anger to be why I'm lonely. To be honest, I am already lonely—let me rephrase, I can't handle your contempt reminding me: *Is this who you want to be sick alongside, Walela?*

I do not have enough to give and also keep my feet moving to make you see me. Maybe not even me, just: my standby heart. Have you not seen it? I've handed over my organs each year. Left my hands as an offering at Degnan. Cut out my tongue too. Made myself the damn court jester and someone I don't recognize at Brynhurst. I know I got bad blood and maybe that's why we are both okay with me spilling it for us in our first apartment at Pinafore. A river of criticism leads me back to you and a labyrinth's dance floor showing up to practice.

I give you my arm, a brittle twig under a steel-toed boot. Cue the music, and Death flips over the hourglass. We both wait for you to step up before the last grain drops.
Can you please come home before I may have to leave you here?
I want you to apologize for showing up so late. Can you say sorry and mean it?
Sorry. For thrusting yourself, your family, and your gossiping and bills on my back, expecting me to carry you all. Keep the truth locked away in your basement. My desire to simply be loved made me invisible to myself at times. Ignore the symptoms. Side effects.

Test results. Don't you get it? Somewhere between when we met and now, I became willing to die for you and your happiness. Crucify myself into your redemption and do all the work in hopes of resurrecting a love I once knew. And by once knew, I mean the girl I made all my pinky promises to about who I am living for: It was you, always you as the answer, when I hated my body for being cancer's mighty temple.

Maybe those bullshit cancer movies are right, maybe we are only good for being the lesson. The one that makes those around us better . . . for someone else, for another life . . . without us. I cannot teach you how to love me this many years in. I cannot love you and also supplement your self-love. I am asking to be chosen. Love me like I am not always going to be here because, my dear, one day you and I will both be a distant memory and the Earth will have never known we were once here.

I do not want to beg, but please be more than an echo reverberating throughout this ballroom like an earthquake. Cue the music. I will ask Death to flip the hourglass. Again. I do not want to dance myself into a bleached skeleton waiting for you to arrive in time. I will keep spinning in my own blood. My suit painting the dance floor as I continue to show up for practice. Learning the steps to be graceful for the both of us.

I do not want to leave you, so please don't make it so I have to. I refuse to promise I will be the same person from when we met but I will be a fire flare. Show you where to meet me again when you are ready. I know, foolish of me to make everything on your own terms. I am a chandelier, flickering, moths collaging themselves over me, yet most do not acknowledge the dimming. Only until the room is dark. Until the sun sets. Until I cannot rise again.

Love, the music can't bring itself to begin, the hourglass just broke into a fault line. The last of my dirty blood is what I've left behind: an island to seep into the floorboards. Death left with the door wide open. Such a shame, the stains. Look at how little we both loved me.

I Already Prepared My Funeral Before
a Pandemic So You All Don't Have To

[a rose-gold urn sitting on the surface
of a single white marble pillar] [the white marble
pillar is erected in one of the last small
Baptist churches in Los Angeles] [a wooden pulpit
to the side encourages the eulogizing]

let there be marigolds drenched in sugar
and flower girls pollinating the floor with them,
the first processional to Orion Sun's "Betterrr."
[know I agree with Orion, I could've been better.
let me do so as a shapeless orb]

transition to a hard pivot with a moment of silence.
there will be no photos of me or black clothing worn.
you are gathered here today to let go of me.
extract the serum of pain and eject it into the air.
say the [spell] psalm / read the passage [story]
allow the preacher to speak [grant the lesson]

open for words of acknowledgment,
curse me into oblivion or hold my last words close:
i tried, i promise i did.

[continue] carry the urn.

the second processional to Rett Madison's "Shame Is a River"

dump me into a body of water
where I can swim in circles.
let all the ashes feed the clouds
and a thunderstorm will rain hail,
rocks of black ice scattering
across Los Angeles. inconvenient
evidence [me: raising hell in heaven]

Curveball

I got a call that I have a donor.
I celebrated. Until I couldn't.
She backed out.
Reasons unknown because of privacy.
Now I gotta sit tight and wait six months.
My whole home packed with a transplant
that had a tentative date. Potential
for what could have been remains consistent.
Disappointment follows me into the backstage
of my mental health. Under the covers of my bed,
I practice the bounce back I know is expected of me.
I been exhausted, tumbling down a valley
of "trusting the process." I stay in bed.
Swearing vehemently at optimism
and fooling myself into convictions like:
My life is special enough to beat any odds.
I know that's not my voice that said that,
but I recall it in my own.
Curveballs shoot out a batting-cage cannon.
I take the hits.
Motionless.
Stoic.

Spirit, if you are listening,

please tell me
there is not a heaven
but a field of lilies.
There is Genesis,
no apple, just us.
Sitting on the ground
as kids. Playing cards,
braiding hair, holding hands,
doing double Dutch and hopscotch,
with barbecue-smoked platters
and side dishes galore.
Black excellence
is not the metric.
A paradise for repose.
Black people
unbothered
in tranquility.

Shaving My Head in My First-Ever Apartment, July 2020

I shaved my head when I learned I had a potential match and donor for my transplant. But it was so much more than that. I remember women lamenting hair loss in my support groups. The trauma of realizing what an illness and its medicine can do. Make us into a toxic hazard and a reminder we are filled with tombstones. I didn't want to remember my hair falling out. I didn't want the scene where I am pulling out my curls on accident in my hospital bathroom. The amount of love we attach to what grows outside of us. The amount of worth and beauty we place on it. Older women have always reached for my hair, talking about how it makes me, me. Imagining out loud about if they had my hair: *"I'd never worry 'bout shit. I'd be shaking my head so much like a bobblehead. Annnddd no, miss, this ain't no wig."* I woke up in July, my apartment filled with humidity and the sun beaming down on our South Central apartment, and I decided I hate being called beautiful. This isn't some "oh, it's so hard to be pretty" shit, this is some "I think people see me as a diet woman when I'm nonbinary" shit. I want to be called stunning and handsome at once. I want to know what I will look like without hair, and I want to create good memories with it. Where I tap my temple and take a mental screenshot to save into my brain. Listen, there are few places I get to exercise choice. You don't have to tell me how my grandmama in heaven is looking down, shaking her head, but sometimes I gotta do what's best for me. Do what makes my body feel less dangerous, less womanly, less of a catchall for everyone's assumptions. I told Ivie to get the clippers while I got the scissors. Sat down in our dining area while listening to random music that I wish I could remember the name of. I tied my hair into a bun, stretched it to the moon, and Ivie, standing over me, sliced the scissors through it. There it was, a ball of 2016 to 2020 in my hands. By the end, I was sitting in a black ring of hair, felt like a summoning circle, felt like I left shit behind, slithered out my body, and hopped into another that I can call my own for a moment. I go into the shower and wash the remnants of hair stuck to the back of my neck and ears away. Watch small memories swirl then dive down the drain. How many people will think I'm having a crisis? We've seen those in the early 2000s. How many people will still see me as a woman, give me some divine feminine compliment? I dry myself off as I look in the mirror. For the first time in my life, I could see my face and all it held in my reflection and I didn't care to answer to anyone but myself. Everything could wait. I will stand naked, humid, with steam rising and falling in this small dilapidated bathroom for a minute. Trace the shape of my face and body. What a brilliant vessel we are through everything that is tempestuous.

Haunted Hill House Follows Us Everywhere

Stevie comes over weekly,
juggling a bucket, mop, magic scrub,
and bleach to help clean what Ivie won't.
Before the lockdown, we'd slide open
the closet door after Ivie told another
one of her lies without consequence.
I don't think those matter to her.
However, I am still expected to care
for her and myself and this leukemia.
I hold myself to the same double
standard Ivie has always benefited from.
I am a replication of the caregivers in my family.
Potential be so intoxicating, but I have a tolerance now.
The apartment humid like
locker rooms outside chlorine pools.
An opulence of mold flourishes.
What was once a small vine
now a fuzz-filled tree
leeching onto what belongs to me
without forethought or care.

"hostage" —Billie Eilish

I am trying to get over it. But I am still plagued
   by imagined gunshots.
Door slams wake me, and the shower steam covers me
   like a heating blanket.
I rock back and forth in a white tub repeating what my
   therapist taught me:
                       "Then is not now, then is not now."

Our front door is unlocked. I got my own set of keys. Same as you.
I am hostage to what you may or may not do if I try to leave again.
You underestimate what your actions can do to people's psyche.
The consequences of this "caregiving" reversing your youth.

I don't think you are ready to be married.
I am not allowed to say it, though.
I am to ask questions but only in good faith.
Tone-check [repress] myself.
So I give you an out, then another. With each ignored promise,
I suggest a friend like: Stevie, stepping in to care.
Or leaving me altogether. You vigorously shake your head.
                                     No.

The whole "in sickness and in health" was a vow to me.
Vows have different meanings to us. See.
I am starting to think for myself now

because I am finally thinking of my own Freedom now.
The dependency of disability does not result in compromise
but rather a heightening of tolerance for pain.
But if you cannot handle the cancer,
Ivie, please allow me to lose you.
Don't hold me hostage to your selfishness.
Keeping me in a corner as the apartment is coated in grease.
Stop waiting until I am no longer defective [I am not,
    I have cancer]
until I am the person you got on one knee for [I am not,
    I am older now]
until all these bad things [cancer] of mine
that you avoid talking about poof into memory
[compartmentalizing].

You forget: back then,
I had cancer running around in my blood on that beach
when you proposed to me. So forgive me for asking:
Do you enjoy my suffering?
Is there power in having someone older than you,
weaker than you? Who cannot fight like you?
Wield a knife or a gun like you? Crack open
a coconut with their bare hands like you?

Help is no longer in my vocabulary.
I've lost my way out of here.
You hid the trapdoor, and now no one can get
in to scrub the negligence. You love the glorification
of being a caregiver, the long social media dedication posts,

but you ain't been with me to the doctor, handled my meds,
handled my appointments, insurance, the bills, phone calls.
It's all so inconvenient. Annoying even. That the cancer
   is mostly ignored.
But. Look at you, a hero, sticking with your pitifully sick partner.
Who knows what will arrest my heart: you   or   the cancer.

There Is No Prescription for Grief

My psychiatrist was frustrated on my behalf today. More so
at my circumstances.
My psychiatrist is one of the few people I don't hide the entirety
of my trauma from.
He knows the hazard lights are blinking when I explain how
alone this is all getting.
The longer I have cancer, the less people know what to say—or
do with it.
It worsens, but the hospitalizations and complications continue,
kind people die,
friendships lost, family gone; it feels empty. It's as if God
struck me down
and I crashed through a marble floor into the first layer of hell.
I now laugh at the idea of being as hopeful as I was even three
years ago. I feel hope chip away each time a friend dies,
each time someone I don't know dies of the same illness, each
time a chemo fails,
each time
I think of the past, each
time, each
time,
each time it gets more unbearable.
I watch the sun rise and hang and set before me, and it's the best
I can do. But that's not living; it's just wandering through it all.
My stomach hosts a tombstone, and I've spent so long running
from death, but

part of having cancer is befriending death as a means of coping.

Lately, the idea of letting go
and walking in his shadow feels easier. Where can I hope to
live when the second I feel okay, there's another set of bruised
knuckles awaiting my cheek to burst? My psychiatrist tells me
he would be more concerned if I didn't feel that way. He offers
me extra medications to possibly flatten out my emotions.
I say no. We agree I should ride this depression. This grief.
All the way out. I keep trying. I write in my journal, I create
alternate realities in video games, I buy too many candles,
I eat cake,
I eat cookies,
I eat ice cream,
I go on my elliptical until I taste my heartbeat.
I buy skincare, but my face breaks out. I buy bright-colored
    clothes, but really, I want to be invisible.
I try to meditate, but it feels pointless. My altar collects dust.
I've learned my lessons. I've learned more than most ever
have to consider. I am a young child kicking their legs,
refusing to go to preschool. I am a newborn wailing to go
back inside my mother. There is no prescription for grief.
Just hold your breath and collect the smallest amount of
hope and the biggest amount of courage so that you can
make it to the other side. Again. Each time asking.
Is it worth it?

Irony Makes One Last Joke—
I Promise It's the Last One

What am I to do
when the world
shows me it will
gladly move on
without me?

A virus that
would kill me
is marketed
as manageable.

Nowhere is safe
like it used to be.
And back then,
it wasn't all
that
safe either.

Hindsight is 20/20
and a thorn in my heel.

All of the last hope
I placed into transplant
for a better life than before.

But Better
is impossible now.
Right now
Society
is collapsing.

What irony.

To endure everything
and receive nothing.

Exploitation in Death

They made Whitney & Tupac
Sambo dance as holograms.
They stole Henrietta's stem cells
and made her live on for eternity.
But we not supposed to linger
in ways outside our consent.
Harriet Cole's nervous system
is an exoskeleton on display
by lying white doctors.
Claimed she was a janitor
without a paper trail.
Convenient. Actin' like.
When we dead,
we not supposed to spiral
beside the cosmogram.
In Birmingham,
a Black girl, Addie Mae,
was bombed to death,
and her remains go missing.
Black bodies archived
for "our" contributions in death.
Generations after are told
by the oppressor that these
immoral, heinous deeds
were "necessary."
"It's for the advancement of humanity,"

yet no consequences.
Spirits who cannot find their way
wander a midnight trail,
squinting their eyes, trying to recall.
But they are in an afterlife
confined to the microscopes
of institutions, their petri dishes,
anatomy labs, artificial intelligence
eternally stuck inside the infinite unknown.

Chemotherapy, Round Three: ICLUSIG

I wake up to a bruise spread out across my upper leg, a supernova, with a lump hidden underneath it. The next day, I wake up to yet another bruise. A small green pebble on my outer left thigh. I call my oncologist. He says to wait four days until the next appointment. So cue my ruminating thoughts, and it's a rodeo for four days.

A bruise is a reminder of the unpredictability of cancer. It's a *"gotcha."* The *"what if this time, this time is the time when the medicine fails."* And it is. I sit in a cramped room at my transplant center with two doctors staring worriedly at my blood test results alongside my oncologist. White blood cells are 78,000. Normal is 10,000. My LVH is 599. Normal is at most 299. My platelets are low. My hemoglobin has dropped. I can keep going. But you get the point. It's not great.

We let out a sigh because we all know this means a second oral chemo has failed. Except this time, unlike the last time, I know my body is not a failure, I know that I am not a failure, a fuckup; my mother doesn't come in my head to tell me what a screwup I am. Everything is quiet, and it just is what it is. There will be no tears this time. There will be no premature musings on death. I have survived myself before, and I will do so again. What is the plan. My oncologist tells me to come back in four days, and in the meantime, I will be put on an old-school oral chemo—three pills, three times a day—same pills I took during my first hospitalization. This will be the intermediary as my transplant center arranges for my new oral chemo, ICLUSIG, to make its way from a post office to my home.

A year ago, I swore to myself I would never take ICLUSIG. I had read the side effects and pushed the computer away from me. Fear engulfed me. Blood clots. Cardiotoxicity. Blindness. I said, *"Nah, I ain't messin' around with that."* My family got enough history with blood clots. My grandmama died that way, and I got enough history with chemo to be skeptical. When my oncologist tells me he's putting me on ICLUSIG, one of my fears comes true. I repeat to him what I told the computer a year ago. For the first time, I have a doctor who understands. Who validates me. Meets me where I am and nudges me gently yet firmly. He talks me through the plan. Maybe he knows I like plans. But it helps. I place my hands over my head and begrudgingly say yes through my mask.

"We are trying to get to transplant; you got less than a month, kid," my subconscious reminds soothingly. *"What did we agree on? You were gonna make it to the starting line even if it meant dragging your body there."*

Well, we doin' it. And this time, I don't curse a God who doesn't love me. Or yell about how my head isn't covered by my ancestors. Instead, I accept it. I say the opposite. I exhale on the long drive home. My lover asks me if I'm okay. I say yes and I mean it. What can I be mad about? I've done everything and then some to keep my body afloat. What is not in my control is not for my will to be done. That's the truth you learn in transplant. No one knows how this is gonna go: not you, not your team, not your donor—you just try. You try to survive it all. There is no control with cancer.

I house a daredevil of an illness, the blast of meteors; I house a hundred stacks of dynamite. I meditate in the middle of a deserted junkyard with eyes closed. Deep breathing. Open my hand. Say: *"Give me the pills. Let's try this again."*

Messages in a Bottle Lost on an Island Shore Somewhere, Part Two

October 19, 2020:

Text Message: To Mom:

Hi Mom, my oncologist thought I should send this.
My pride has been a mound of prewritten texts now
getting lost in my notes app. We thought I had a donor
for my transplant, that one in tens of millions. She agreed
but then backed out. It feels like no one really cares about
living as much as I do, but I guess I should expect that.
No one cares about you more than you care about you.
You taught me that one: *"Nobody's got me like I got me"*
has been getting me through. But my oncologist suggested
family members may be better matches. You don't have to
talk to me or have anything to do with me, I promise.
I just really need this transplant.

November 6, 2020:

Text Message: To Mom:

I just got an email, and two more donors were found,
which is lucky. One is in Brazil, the other is in Greece.
My oncologist said we'll be proceeding with the lady
from Greece. She agreed too. So fingers crossed those
stem cells fly into the cryo chamber at City of Hope.
I'm sorry I disturbed you. I'll be admitted to their
transplant unit in December. My immune system
replaced and maybe we can all move on from cancer.

You and me included.
I hope you are okay.
I miss you. Always.

Turns Out My Mother Didn't Block My Number

<u>November 7, 2020:</u>
<u>Text Message: From Mom:</u>
I miss you.
I love you.
Always.
I am so sorry.
You are stronger
than I ever was.
I found some
photos of you,
I want you
to have them.
Remember
I am always
proud of you.

Call me when
you get a chance.

My Donor

A nameless, faceless thirty-five-year-old woman
in Greece agrees to give me her immune system.
A stranger agrees to become a part of me
without knowing me. And just me,
needing a transplant, is enough.
No begging or pleading with her
directly on the internet.
A "sure thing" is not what I am used to,
so I tread suspiciously, lightly.
I heard on *Grey's Anatomy*
when you've experienced so much trauma,
even the best things will feel just as doom-inspiring.
My caseworker suggests I write a card anonymously.
I write in cursive on cheap stationery
about how I don't know if thank-you is enough.
I wanted to write, *"A part of me quietly wishes*
we are related." When tracing my genealogy,
I saw some of my family lived in Athens, Texas,
and I cocked my head to the left, wondering
if my whole life was planned out before I even arrived,
or if I am using philosophy to make meaning out of coincidence:
a woman who is my guardian angel agreed to give me
another shot at bull-riding life. Maybe it's none of the above.

And something simple. Like a stranger's selflessness keeps me alive. No epic coincidence. No parable. No greater meaning. Just a woman. Saying yes. Emphatically. To the idea of me.

the grand exile

Cancer,
on the theatrical
stage of social media,
makes you a handheld,
portable spectacle.

The spotlight fades when
a donor is found.
The aisles exile thousands
bored with the prospect
of remission
being more plausible,
now unsatisfied and
filling out exit surveys
at the unfollow button
on my Instagram page.

Rating my page at: 4 out of 10.
Reviews read as follows:

"I wanted to watch
with suspense for longer."
"I was hoping they'd die."

"I knew them; no,
I didn't reach out."

"I gossiped with
my friends about them."
"I sort of enjoy
watching tragedy passively."

"I dunno, they kinda
no longer left me
mystified;
they became
. . . normal."

The Hickman as My Last Tattoo Session

Cocooned on top of a metal slab, tinfoil-wrapped like a
    take-out burrito,
I lie in an operating room. Tied at the shoulders, all my limbs
    stiff in place.
The fentanyl is not "the same silly juice" the doctor
    and nurses promised.
I am known to *not* accept what soothes me, so this development
    is rather unsurprising.
Like this was definitely not the part in *Euphoria* when Rue licked
    the liquid fentanyl off
the knife held by a tattooed drug dealer in Fez's crib. The
    absolute need for it immediately
after the comedown. I fixated on potential drugs used in the
    stem cell transplant guide they
give every patient—fentanyl, in blue print, made the list, and
my already small veins shifted in discomfort. Rue knocks
and slams at Fez's door. They push another dose.
Eyes are all that talk in a room full of masks. Three doses.
Still nothing. Nurse A is likely questioning if I've done
this before. For consolation: The freckle-looking track marks
on my arms are from botched blood draws and IVs. Nurse B
gives me a concerned look, then to Nurse C, who is
unamused. Do I actually know what they are thinking?
Absolutely not.
I'm at the hospital, though, so I'm supposed to assume
    the worst of myself.

Lidocaine beestings three times, pinches my chest with a small
    needle, and my chest
becomes tough dough to knead. A catheter ropes into the
    right side of my chest
and I look at the operating room's left wall. Unflinching.
    The tube claw cranes
and connects to the right vein. Two stitches open a portal to the
    very thing that betrays
us eventually: the heart. *"I made sure to keep it away from the
    'be joyous' you have*
so it won't scar," the doctor says affectionately.
Scars are but varying memories, Doc, tattoos included.
But I grin instead. *"Be joyous"* and *"(Be)loved"* on each clavicle
are five-year-old reminders now, my private euphoria.
Weightless scribblings of a twenty-two-year-old who found pain
and Toni Morrison in a wine bottle. I'm older now.
I let the surgeon slice my body and snatch the scalpel out
    from my hands.
Pretend he is a heavy-handed tattoo gun.
He seals the catheter with Saran Wrap that holds all the blood,
slimy from aftercare, and siphons out the wound
    with warm water.
A burgundy caterpillar trails in a downward spiral to
    the sink's bottom,
and I stand, wanting to be a god commanding leukemia to leave.

My Last Night with Riley

I contemplate Death as Riley sleeps beside me.
She once pocketed herself into my hair and shoulders.
Now it's the curve of my legs. Ties herself into a knot. And sleeps.
Dreams. Gallops. Wags her tail. She is spirited and of the mighty.
I always question, *"Riley, have you been here before?*
Cuz it sure in the hell feels like it." She cocks her head to the right
answering no, to the left answering yes. She does not answer
that question
but will pick up a command like, *"Bring me your toy"* in one try.
So instead, I ask: *"Do you want to go outside, do you want a treat?*
Show me what you need." This child, dog, otherworldly being
has got the vocabulary of what feels like a four-year-old running
like a fool through the house. But will sit with such
    a mature stillness
for the promise of a Milk-Bone. Or will pant underneath
    a burning daylight,
showing off her saber-toothed canines fully capable of more
    damage than imaginable.
She pants and grins and whines at sunset. When morning
    yawns at dusk,
one last time, we sit on the balcony, shoulder to shoulder.
Both enthralled by a peach sky and its Studio Ghibli clouds.

Highway to Transplant

Google Maps has us take the "long" way, the "scenic" route. In Los Angeles, that translates to: *Why is there so much traffic?* A gray wagon filled with my life (books, clothes, photos, a projector, and every remedy for anything related to chemo and radiation) rattles in the back seat of Ivie's small car. We drive through the Figueroa Street Tunnel. An archway of metallic stone with grass and modern industrialization covering it. I hold my breath like I used to in the back seat of my parents' car driving home from El Segundo. I claim this is a test of my "pulmonary function." I use tests when I am uncertain. The internet got a quiz for everything. Apparently, I am Tanjiro from *Demon Slayer* and Megumi from *Jujutsu Kaisen*. I proctor quizzes of my own: Can you do a mile on the elliptical in less than eleven minutes? When the answer is no, then, to me, it means transplant will fail.

How long can you hold your breath for? The standards I've started to hold myself to can be impossible, despite having been cleared for transplant by far more accurate testing. A green check mark next to my body said that it was ready for all the hell to come. But that's not enough certainty for me. Tests in high school determined the semester, which meant the future. I used to calculate how much could go wrong for me to still get an A. Tests, for me, become an equation. I can swim through a transplant if I can swim into a cave with an opening as wide as the Figueroa Tunnel, kick ferociously, and avoid getting drowned by my saliva.

I flip a quarter. Heads means I die, and tails means I get to go home. Twelve hawks circle ahead in a clear sky, and each represents an omen. I am trying to stop looking for the future on this drive. Slap my hand with a wooden ruler that leaves splinters. For two hours, I repeat: *I don't know how any of this transplant will go. I am at the whim of Spirit, fate, destiny, the universe.* Downtown Los Angeles moves out of my eyesight in the rearview mirror like Stevie's "You Got This" posters did earlier, before I got on the freeway. This is my last time seeing my city for who knows how long.

Going back home means two very different things as we drive into City of Hope's empty parking lot. I cross the threshold of Helford Hospital as the sun falls asleep behind me. I am doing this alone because safety is in solitude during a pandemic. There are no answers. No predictions. No variables unveiling themselves early. No wisdom. Merely pleading with Harmony that I can float in the bottomless unknown. Let it all go unanswered. I don't know when or if I'm gonna get outta this place. There's no cartomancy, Diloggun reading, throwing of dice and bones that can dictate when a body will hiccup. It's not a failure if this doesn't work. It's not a failure.

I did enough. I did better than good. I did great.

Dear God,
Please let me have the smoothest,
safest, easiest transplant
and recovery known to humankind.

—*You Gotta Be Specific with Prayers*
to Close up the Loopholes

Compared to the oral chemo pills,

intravenous chemo is . . . uneventful.
No churning out tonight's dinner,
no burst vessels, no inflammation.
I simply have lost my taste for anything
except what is bitter.
—*chemo kills everything except . . .*

My Granny and I Both Do Transplant Together Cuz We Both Have (Had) Leukemia:

When my grandma died, I was thirteen years old. I was never the same, but someone did make sure I wouldn't lose myself in the mourning: her sister, Jennie. I affectionately called her Granny even though she was my great-aunt. She knew her home was where I needed to settle in on the weekends.

In the hours before church on Sunday morning, I'd watch my granny pick from a wide assortment of hats with intricate faux floral arrangements and colorful dresses. But on Sundays, she always wore white. She was known as a Mother at Little Zion Baptist Church. This was the first place I really saw God move in Black people in ways I had never seen. From gospel to praise dance to worship sermons. I'd sit in the front row with her and the other Mothers. All older Black women, all dressed in various textures of white: silk, sequined, bedazzled, knitted, cotton, or polyester. They made the all-white WORK every Sunday. She'd slide me those barrel-shaped mints that feel foamy as they disintegrate on your tongue. At night, we'd watch Discovery Channel, WWE, and Food Network. She'd lean into a reclining chair while I'd either sit on one of her floral armchairs or the couch wrapped in clear plastic. One night, the air was thick and morose, and I asked why she didn't seem to cry about her sister—my grandma—being gone. She said, *"I know Mary is in a better place; she's not hurting. I miss her, but she's not in pain, baby."* We sleepily allowed our eyes to close beside each other in bed. She was healing. Just her presence alone.

In eleventh grade, what was supposed to be a quick ER trip became ten months in the hospital, my mother working around the clock to ensure my granny's care and comfort. "I Trust You" by James Fortune & FIYA played one day in the hospital room, and Granny started weeping. Mother jumped to her side, asking what was wrong. Nothing was wrong. She knew it was her time to go. She had done her job: I was okay, Mama was okay, Auntie was okay. It was time to go home. And she did.

There have been murmurs among family members about Granny having had leukemia and it returning before she died. All news to me. I sink into my bed the same way she sank into her armchair. Ask for gospel music to be played out of my red mini speaker. It's hard to explain, but she was there. With my grandma and papa. My holy trinity. Hovering behind my bed. Ensuring my heart kept pumping, my lungs kept releasing air, and my eyes opened and smiled. We all knew it could've been the end; it was projected to be the end by doctors right then and there, but the four of us. Refused. Knowing it doesn't take the Second Coming of Christ to produce a miracle.

total-body radiation

Two peach steps.
A passageway to step through.
Two molded shields of my lungs,
shining like nickels,
remain propped against a glass,
and stickers with Sharpie stuck
onto my collarbones and back
measuring proportions that cannot
be washed off. Two sessions a day.
Eight in total. A large cannon points
at the entirety of my bones.
A ring of lasers points at my stem cells.
The lights shut off.
My red pants and patterned blue gown
disappear—my back straightens.
No lotion, no jewelry, no moving allowed.
I balance my weight on handlebars sticking
out beside my waist, and I am petrified wood,
standing still for fifteen minutes.
Lightning crackles:
stay to the front,
okay, turn your back,
okay, now up close: the ribs,
a tickle of cancer being electrocuted.

There's no squeal of laughter,
rather me, as the Vitruvian Man,
near perfect in anatomy:
empty of cells.

"If you want to have some of the best chances of getting out this hospital, if you can, walk. Every single day."

—Almost every nurse and doctor at City of Hope

Walker, Meet Walker Mathews

The transplant unit got hallways bent to the shape of a horse track. Nursing stations on one, with various colored scrubs stacking on top of each other to look over at a computer screen or a patient's chart. On the opposite side, patient rooms. Some keep their doors open and you catch a glimpse of who they are, what their room looks like, how sick they are, and others, fatigued, sit in darkness. The patients don't have anybody here. It's a pandemic after all.

My first night unpacking the wagon, a man twice my age with hunched shoulders, wearing a fleece zip-up and a Darth Vader– lookin' mask, zoomed by my window more times than I cared to count. My first full day, I woke up to the same familiar silhouette passing by.

My oncologist visits my room as I'm standing on top of a blue armchair while attempting to hang a tapestry, like this hospital room is gonna look anything like a real room. He does his usual, *"Heeellllooooooo,"* in a deep voice, always smiling at however he finds me when I'm left to my own devices. *"You know, if you want to get out of here, you've got to—"* *"Walk,"* I interrupt. Lap. I got it. You don't gotta tell me twice cuz I, too, am trying to get the hell up outta here.

I fasten a KN95 mask on before making rounds and rounds around. Kicking my IV pole ahead and catching up with a fast stride, making a game of leapfrog. Early 2000s hip hop blasting from my portable speaker. Dependent on the time of day, you might get some classical.

It is the holiday season, though, so you definitely gon' get some Boyz II Men, Destiny's Child, TLC–type of Christmas songs. I'm the DJ of the unit. The youngest here. Honey, I knew comin' in that it was about to be all old, mostly white men, but we all wakin' up and walkin' today. Competitiveness keeps boredom at bay, so in the less-than-twenty-four hours I've been in the hospital, I calculated eight rounds equals a mile. Multiply that by two, three, or five. You're good. Make it to ten thousand steps or as close to, and you doin' real good.

It hasn't been ten days, but almost every nurse has seen me rushing by. Actin' like I got some place to be. And I do. Up outta here. They sing to the music playing or cheer me on from the sidelines as I get various bright-colored charms added to the army chain around my neck: one for each mile. My nickname affectionately becomes "The Walker" instead of "Patient in Room #____."

Got the same nickname as my second great-grandfather: "Walker" Mathews. The first time we meet, he appears at dusk. I am in a long-standing meditation when I step out my room. Social media don't matter. Phone on do not disturb. Slip on black, gray, and white Nikes with *222* embroidered on the back like a football player's jersey. Walker floats beside me until we reach the end of the hall and go to turn around.

We talk about San Augustine, Freedom Colonies in Texas, and

Justice Precinct 1. He shares that he was born in 1874, and we walk an entire lap as we do the math on our hands together to measure how many years separate us. *"Mama—Eliza, her name— had three girls and five boys. My siblings. And we stayed close together. That's our best accomplishment: the family stayed together, and then the family I made stayed together. People don't realize how special that is, you know?"*

I tell him about Los Angeles being too expensive and how I may retreat to the mountains like Octavia said in *Parable of the Sower* but feel bad for not making it work. One morning, he thrusts out his hands, calloused from farming. *"That's city life. You not made that way. You got it in you to be out in that field. I like that Earthseed; go way up in that mountain."*

When I ask him about Reconstruction one morning, he stops. *"You know your auntie Susan, yeah, she my mama's mama's sister. She can talk way more 'bout that. Oh yeah, she done visited you in one of your dreams, huh? You can't move, and she come in talking about it smell or what got to get cleaned. She came over a lot, in our sleep, she love some you though. She taught me about the—what's it called, the month you're born in with the stars?"* "Zodiac." *"Yeah, yeah, when you was gone and wasn't callin' on us no more, I told myself, 'Imma go keep up with the kids; that way if I do meet you, we got stuff to talk about. I can tell you things, like I'm a Taurus."*

I joke about how with that knowledge, he and my Pisces ass would've been laid up like Jennie and Mary watching TV and eating food we were not supposed to. *"Uh-uh-uh, we would NOT*

be. Idle mind is a devil's workshop; that's why I'm out here walkin'
beside you, telling these stories.

"We never got a house, no land, nothin', but I said my daddy was
born in Alabama, my mama in Texas, and I said we ain't moving
a damn step. I stayed plowing in the fields. That's how it was; you
didn't question it. . . . I ain't ever got to do nothin' new. You the first
who got somethin' to say, got them hard fingertips from playin'
that guitar and writing those poems. We all been askin' who you
got the music bone from. Some of your ancestors are still tryna
find you, always are. But lotta us be waiting to come see you, long,
long line. We can't come all at once, but I said, 'They called the
great-great-grandaddy with that nickname 'Walker.' I'm comin',
I'm on my way."

I can tell he's embarrassed to not have more to give me. "I get
sad cuz I wish I paid attention to my mama too, my grandmama.
Maybe I'd have some more, but funny thing, the more years go by,
the more I forget. . . . I almost missed the train ride when Mary
and Jennie left here and went to Los Angeles, and now I'm here
in—what's this place called?" "Duarte." "Duarte! You know I can't
speak all that well." "You ain't gotta explain yourself, Grandaddy
Walker."

His face transforms into a young boy's, one I don't think ever got
to hear that, and gasps. We stay quiet for the rest of the laps, and
we both don't mind it. By the seventh one, he starts getting into
formation like a sprinter waiting for the pistol shot at the Olympics.

"I said I was coach. Race yuh back, lil one."

Before I lurch forward, he becomes the abrupt closing of a door, a gush of wind, and he jet-streams into my Bible, perched on a porch in Proverbs. Waiting until I go to open the door again. Stepping out onto the track.

Walking.

"High" by Miley Cyrus, of All Things, Makes Me Cry in the Transplant Unit

Lavender kisses pastel pink behind mountains outside my window.
My chunky black headphones block out all noise except for a guitar
strumming in the F key and Miley Cyrus moodily crooning about
a lover who no longer visits her dreams. She yearns for someone
she is not sure she misses, and I reach toward my lover
and wonder the same. I panic in an empty hospital room
and howl for the first time. Yes, lover, I am betraying you.
I sing along and question if this is worth it.
Your promise of potential crowding my common sense.
Should've known at the trauma dumping, at the "I love you"
after mere days of meeting. I believed it because I was so delighted
to be wanted, finally, wholly, for the first time in my life.
"What would you do if I got a ring and proposed to you?"
I said yes, our limbs Jenga'd between each other,
and I was a doll designed to fit into your embrace.
In the isolation of a transplant unit,
I am comprehending your absence.
I am not worth your time. But. My hands refuse to write
the poem I need to. With rounded shoulders,
my tears lament the future I once saw for us.
The sky is a shadow, and everything is blank.
I am fervently searching for the logic behind love.
Miley sings that comfortability will conceal itself as security,
so what are you really lookin' for, baby?
I wipe my pink swollen eyes, lightly touch the bandage

covering my Hickman line. Maybe, if the cancer leaves,
maybe that apathetic side of my lover will rip itself
out and walk out the hospital with the leukemia.
I did agree to forever. I did promise my best.
In sickness and in health. Lover,
you haven't met me in health.

Future Me Meets My Younger Self Before the Cancer:

After "Make You Proud" by Jensen McRae

The slow expansion of bruising is not to be ignored.
The aluminum tin rattle of a cough is not to be ignored.
Sweats of the night, tender lumps under the skin,
a jutted-out abdomen marking a distended spleen,
the bone pain when walking are not to be ignored.
But you will ignore it all.
Know that you are a walking corpse.
Made it to the ER just in time to be told:
"You are likely outta time."
I wish I still had your unabashed naivety
reducing the mountain of mortality to a small skipping stone,
chucking it across a river and choosing to still push forward.

The diagnosis is real.
It will take you almost three years to accept.
You will see love walk out the hospital with you.

You are not told this enough, so I'll do it on behalf of everyone:
the best thing about you is your fierce compassion.
You are so invested in autonomy, yet it'll still be stripped away.
By different doctors. Fatphobic oncologists. Racist hospital staff.
Somehow you were made for it.
To ride the wave just like the fearless child
did in Maui, boogie-boarding and free-diving.

You will ignore the abuse.

You will make excuses

because to not be loved is to not exist at all.

I can say I don't know how we made it

—but we did. I think it was the me now,

holding on to you in the moment back then,

holding on to little you

who'd dance in ice-cream shops,

cannonball into pools,

pet dolphins at SeaWorld while

behaviorists weren't watching.

Oh, sweet one, you always knew you deserved it all.

Something encourages me to give thanks to our holy trinity

—the way they stood by your bed through everything

    that should've killed us.

Forget a cat with nine lives; we are so committed to this one

there'll be no "Out, out, brief candle" tonight.

Even though you will consider over and over letting

    the cancer overflow

like excess champagne into your bloodstream—

    an honorable suicide

—and it'll be years before you see the abuse, before you name it,

before you deem the replication of confusion is not love.

The replication of neglect is not love.

It is almost torture, for all versions of yourself

have felt this and said, *"Never again,"* so many times.

I hope you remember what Zora warned.

That you won't be silent about the things trying to kill you,

even if you love(d) those things.
You will name your abuser eventually, and the most justice
is a painful awareness. Make peace with that now.

Know a pandemic will come, causing all corners of your hospital
room to try and meet in the middle, smashing you alive.
Transplant is not the fix-all. So.
Find more reasons to live than just living.
Just living will not be enough.
Just surviving will not be enough.
It will be the worst time.
You will carry total-body radiation
as two lung-plate butterfly wings on your back.
A heart-shaped scar where the chemo is infused.
You will carry a body you are still learning
the aftermath of unbecoming.

Do not ignore a single thing that fries your nervous system.
A high tolerance for pain does not mean: ignore.
So do not think about the potential hospital bill
or how you can't afford to be sick.
Young one, you can't afford to play with cancer,
your marrow, leukemia's winning lottery ticket.
The invincibility of youth makes you forget
disability don't give a fuck about youth. Age.
Anything. So. Remember that quote about
our ancestors having seen the apocalypse over and over.
You are still here. And the apocalypse is at dawn.

You are diagnosed. In a way. You do die.

You will apologize to yourself more often.

You will confront the menacing self-talk barking:

you deserve to be the devil's replacement.

Yesterday, we pulled the Queen of Swords tarot card.

A lone wolf with a dagger

protecting all that is tender and precious.

You will go through treatment mostly alone.

Will speak the same language as the doctors,

and that still won't mean it'll translate to: care.

You will be your own nurse, insurance rep,

patient advocate, and caregiver for years.

You will lose who you thought to be the love of your life.

Your love will know devastation in a way that fractures your whole.

And I know right now, you won't believe me because

    she is everything,

but I promise a bigger love is coming,

and you're gonna realize it to Alanis Morissette's

    "Head Over Feet."

You'll realize it's me talking to you.

And you will take that heavy dagger out your sternum,

hand it before Spirit while breathing out all that is true,

surrendering to the scream of salvation:

You saved yourself.

Mary Meets Mary

I unwrap a lollipop,
ready for the odorous
garlic taste of stem cells
everyone warned me about.
An older white woman
with aquamarine eyes
and sandy-blonde hair
exclaims, *"All right,*
we are just about
ready to do a transplant!"

I smile, silent for once.
What do we say
in moments like this?
But it's gotta be
something profound, right?
Yeah, nah, it's all lost on me
as the Benadryl kicks in.
My donor's stem cells
are wheeled to my room
from the cryo chamber
they were preserved in.
My stem cells flew
on a private plane to get
here and remain guarded
in a locked white box.

Inside lie three bags
of what looks like ketchup.
One by one, held up high
on the IV pole. One bag
at a time swings higher
than my other medication,
draining micafungin
and heparin into my system.
They do this so the cells
can have enough momentum
to plunge into my Hickman line.

The same nurse approaches
my bedside. "I'm Mary."
I extend my left arm outward,
and the drawbridge from my elbow leads
to a large flower tattoo on my hand.
The name Mary inscribed thinly atop
my thumb. *A pause.*
        "Well, I guess she's here then."

The clasp is released,
and a slow, scalding
steam rolls from my feet,
shooting up and out my ears.
My Hickman
fills with glittering
scarlet stem cells.
By the window,
Grandma Mary sits

in my room's easy chair.
Holding a ragged Bible,
her face not visible
as she prays in a tan straw hat
like the one she used to wear
with an aquamarine linen dress.

Nurse Mary lets me
murmur Psalm 91.
My grandma and I
raise our heads
at the same time.
For a millisecond,
she tips her hat
and winks.
"Baby,
you gon' be all right.
You gon' be just fine."

Heaven Is at Grandma's House

I enter heaven, and The Spinners play on repeat.
My grandma Mary sways side to side to "I'll Be Around"
—turns to face me, her hair combed into a low bun,
pearls wrapped around her neck, with an all-white dress on.
Her face always carrying a glimpse of a smile.
She is young again. It's her heaven after all.

In the corner I see her sister, Jennie,
the only other woman I called granny.
Got their names tattooed on my left hand
so when you meet me, you get all of them.

My grandma was a woman who
gave birth to children late in life.
A shame she was until her body
could produce what proved her
"womanhood": children.
Once, she was a kid picking cotton
under the unforgiving Texan heat.
Then, turned Los Angeles mother.
Oh, she wanted to be a mother so badly.
Had two kids and did everything she could
to prepare them for a world that does not love us.

Would cuss under her breath but still hold that Bible.
Read The Daily Bread. Make sure the kids were fed,

who wore clothes how they wanted by way of her sewing kit.
Would smoke cigarettes in the bathroom until one of the kids
(my mother) asked, *"Why do you do that!?"* and she said,
   "You know it's bad when the babies start asking questions."

She, who I inherited my true hands from.
Would make mosaics in the back house garage.
Took what was broken and put it together
and that type of reverence for hope
is not to be undermined.

As she got older, she relied on her children,
and they relied on her, and she'd say,
"God loves a child who got their own,"
like in that one Billie Holiday song.
Meaning this world don't give a damn
about Black dreams or Black survival.
But there is a God, and some ancestors
lookin' down or standing beside us,
nudging our backs, and holding our hands,
moving us in the direction we need to be goin'.
Whenever there was mourning,
she'd hum, *"Thy will be done,"*
a calm in calamity,
for my grandmother done
seen revelations more times
than I will ever know.

It's wondrous she made it to the morning I was born.
I exploded into a Cedars-Sinai delivery room,

and the church said amen. Hallelujah.
A child of God. A child of Mercy.
A child of Mary gave birth to a child
who now carries the final legacy.

I was born, and then my fertility died.
The older I get, the more I understand her.
How she held my aunt's hand after
a miscarriage and reminded,
*"We come from a line of strong women,
don't you forget that."*

I honor that I am the last blood-borne legacy.
The other side of hope. A child grown up
can now lie out an altar. Spray the holy water.
Let the sandalwood incense burn.
I am the grown-up child who knows what music
she wants played to commemorate the day
she evaporates into a memory.
She made sure I was a child
who could recite the psalms
because they too are poems,
they too are spells.

Her favorite meal? Tomato soup
and a grilled cheese sliced diagonally.
Dessert? Anything sweet. Except pumpkin pie.
A small milk maiden lies on her side of the altar,
a blue-and-ivory porcelain figurine.
She had an appreciation for what a being's mind could create.

So I call my writing a mosaic of words. I fix the coffee.
Lay out the snacks. Light the white candle.
Kneel and pray. Kneel and read a bookmarked
Psalm 78 from her Bible. Maroon with her name imprinted.
I hug it. Wear a pearl bracelet. Wear her gold-chain bracelet.
I say thank you. I cry.

Fifteen years later. I still cry. Remember thirteen years old
and being in New York for spring break. She told me
she'd be there when I got back. And she tried to be.
She really did. But I like to believe
she left her body before I returned
so I wouldn't have to see anything
but her spirit visit in my dreams.

I am the last child. The last of the Flowers.
Her funeral was the first time I felt I had something
worthwhile to say. And so I did.
Made the room exhale with laughter
about the good times.

She is my legacy as I am hers.
And so if that is really true,
I wish to be half as tender as her.
A quarter as compassionate as her.
If I am anywhere near as resilient,
then my god,
didn't we do a good job then?
Didn't we raise the child right?

So when it's my turn to push
them doors to heaven open,
I will be laid to rest beside her,
just as I decided in that 2017 hospital bed.
And yes,
I know I said *not now* to cancer,
but Life comes for us all.
So when that day comes,
lay me beside the first unconditional,
true love I have ever known.
The alchemy of a Black
grandmother and grandchild.
I will step out my coffin
and onto that dance room floor.
She, the only woman
I will wear my Sunday best for.
Will don mother-of-pearl for.
Will cup her bracelet ready
to return back onto her wrist.

Her sister will say,

> *"Mary, look!"*

My grandmother will spatter out,

> *"Jennie, what now?"*

But she will turn around
with eyes shimmering
like two misty ponds.

No tears, but enough to say,

> *"I've missed you.*
> *I've missed you so much."*

I will smile.

> *"I told you I'd make it eventually."*

She'll reply,

> *"Right on time."*

Crawling Toward the Sky

after "The Rose That Grew from Concrete,"
Tupac Shakur & Nikki Giovanni

Remorse ain't for the cowardly.

Forgiveness be a guillotine for some.

Everyone wants to be the sky,

but no one wants to be cradled by the ground.

Be a rose born from concrete.

People say I got too many thorns.

I say I swallowed the blues and spit fire.

You should try it sometime.

But they don't. So I stopped asking.

I've let a lot of questions die that way.

If they were carcasses,

my mind would be a butcher's dream.

I still don't forgive easy.

I'll throw fists out my mouth.

I ask to be alone most of the time.

There is a difference between alone and lonely.

Loneliness is more of an apology.

I stopped apologizing when I got cancer.

Said big man upstairs broke my hourglass

so I don't got time to cater to egos.

Forgot how to tiptoe four years ago.

Now I'm a heavy-footed ballerina,

and I can still dance so damn well.

I don't call anything I have done

to "get the diagnosis" a mistake
just as regret is a fork in the road
—choices I've made be the same.
All roads lead to Rome,
but I see Rome burning.
I am a chariot of smoke,
the one who doesn't get swallowed by fire.
I been here so many times tryna get this right.
I am the ground. A black rose birthed from despair.
All my previous lives ballroom-dance
as entangled roots, and the blossoming still unfolds.
Damn it. Look here, I ain't dead yet.
Just crawling toward the sky.

"What is there possibly left for us to be afraid of, after we have dealt face to face with death and not embraced it? Once I accept the existence of dying as a life process, who can ever have power over me again?"

—*Audre Lorde,* The Cancer Journals

For every Black patient who didn't make it out of the belly of the beast that is the American healthcare system. For every Black patient who is still out here trying to survive it.

Further Reading

Medical Apartheid: The Dark History of Medical Experimentation on Black Americans from Colonial Times to the Present by Harriet A. Washington

The Cancer Journals by Audre Lorde

A Burst of Light: and Other Essays by Audre Lorde

"10 Principles of Disability Justice" by Sins Invalid

Anarcha Speaks: A History in Poems by Dominique Christina

Capitalism and Disability: Selected Writings by Marta Russell

Illness As Metaphor by Susan Sontag

Between Two Kingdoms: A Memoir of a Life Interrupted by Suleika Jaouad

The Immortal Life of Henrietta Lacks by Rebecca Skloot

Disability Visibility: First-Person Stories from the Twenty-First Century edited by Alice Wong

Care Work: Dreaming Disability Justice by Leah Lakshmi Piepzna-Samarasinha

Ace: What Asexuality Reveals About Desire, Society, and the Meaning of Sex by Angela Chen

Refusing Compulsory Sexuality: A Black Asexual Lens on Our Sex-Obsessed Culture by Sherronda J. Brown

Another Black Girl Miracle by Tonya Ingram

Acknowledgments

Nothing would be possible without my ancestors, guides, Spirit/God/Most High, and so I can't begin anything without acknowledging that.

Katherine, you saw (and continue to see) so much in me during a time I was lost about where I was meant to contribute as a writer, as an artist, and as a thinker. You have pushed me and supported me to be able to stand up, share my life, and say: *I am worthwhile, my writing is worthwhile, so listen up.* Thank you for always being there and available—especially during my frequent spells of random questions.

Sydnee and Kokila, nothing will ever take away from how special this process has been. Thank you for understanding so much of what I desired was something I was once equally fearful of: being honest with myself in ways that commanded grief, mourning, introspection, and connecting with my own history on an even deeper level: with my pen. Thank you for taking a chance on me and for your unending patience.

Elizabeth Velasquez, I used to say frequently, "All I need is for someone to believe in me, show me to a door, unlock it, and I'll handle the rest." Thank you for seeing that, seeing my writing, and knocking on Katherine's door for me to step through.

My friends, you all have given me empathy, have watched and aided my growth, and have seen the vast twists and turns in my life in ways that I never thought would be possible. You each know who you are, no matter if we are friends presently, were friends in the past, or Death interrupted our time together here—I love you all, no matter what, and your love kept me alive many days.

Mom, thank you for bringing me into this world. While our relationship is our own and complicated and cannot be understood in one book alone, I thank God each day that we made our way back to each other. I love you. Endlessly.

Thank you, Leila Steinberg and Mic Sessions, for reminding me I could still write through what I was avoiding and that honesty with self in art reigns above all else.

Cancer Support Community, you have provided help as a facility to so many cancer patients, caregivers, family members, and those experiencing bereavement. Thank you for facilitating the creative writing group that saved me over and over and during my most critical moments, uncorking the ability for me to not only write on what I was going through but also say how I was feeling out loud. Eternally thankful that these programs exist with professionals who understand the complexity of cancer.

Joyce, you were one of my biggest advocates and someone who saw this donor search as something far bigger than just about myself but a community of underserved people; two polar opposites we are, but together we did make something so special.

Eternal gratitude to City of Hope for carrying me to the finish line and giving me a quality of care that I had never experienced before but every patient should be able to experience. Thank you for helping me trust those who provided and continue to provide my medical care—they have done nothing but ensure my best interest, at all times.

Thank you to every therapist and counselor I have worked with, whether in support groups or one on one. I would not be able to understand, verbalize, or share half of what is in this book without encountering each and every one of you.

Thank you to the faculty and workshop staff of my first ever fellowship: Kay Uladay Barrett, Saleem Hue Penny, Raymond Antrobus, L. Lamar Wilson, Meg Day, and fellows alike. Thank you for instilling a safe environment where I felt so held and loved.

Thank you to Writing Coven. It has been an honor to facilitate and watch y'all's growth, love, and support for each other. It has changed me as a person, as a writer, and as a mentor. Each of you rock my world.

Those who have followed this journey from the exact moment I was diagnosed to now or who joined the journey midway through, thank you for always going up for me. I materially would not have survived anything without you all's deep love for me. That cannot go unnoticed or without the utmost regard. I do not take y'all's love for me lightly.